WHITE PRIVILEGE AND BLACK RIGHTS

WHITE PRIVILEGE AND BLACK RIGHTS

The Injustice of U.S. Police Racial Profiling and Homicide

Naomi Zack

ROWMAN & LITTLEFIELD
Lanham • Boulder • New York • London

Published by Rowman & Littlefield
A wholly owned subsidiary of The Rowman & Littlefield Publishing
Group, Inc.
4501 Forbes Boulevard, Suite 200, Lanham, Maryland 20706
www.rowman.com

Unit A, Whitacre Mews, 26-34 Stannary Street, London SE11 4AB

British Library Cataloguing in Publication Information Available

Library of Congress Cataloging-in-Publication Data

Zack, Naomi, 1944-
White privilege and black rights : the injustice of U.S. police racial profiling and homicide /
Naomi Zack.
pages cm
Includes bibliographical references and index.
ISBN 978-1-4422-5055-0 (cloth : alk. paper) -- ISBN 978-1-4422-5057-4 (pbk. : alk. paper)
-- ISBN 978-1-4422-5056-7 (electronic)
1. Racial profiling in law enforcement--United States. 2. African Americans--Civil rights. I.
Title.
HV7936.R3Z33 2015
363.2'308900973--dc23
2015001780

♾ ™ The paper used in this publication meets the minimum requirements of American National Standard for Information Sciences Perma-
nence of Paper for Printed Library Materials, ANSI/NISO Z39.48-1992.

Printed in the United States of America

In Memoriam:
Oscar Juliuss Grant III (1985-2006),
Trayvon Martin (1995-2012),
Eric Garner (1970-2014),
Michael Brown (1996-2014),
Tamir Rice (2002-2014),
among others.

Whereas it is essential, if man is not to be compelled to have recourse, as a last resort, to rebellion against tyranny and oppression, that human rights should be protected by the rule of law.

-–Preamble, Universal Declaration of Human Rights, United Nations, 1948

CONTENTS

PREFACE

Trayvon Martin, Michael Brown, Eric Garner, Tamir Rice, and many others. *"Hands up, don't shoot, Black Lives Matter, I can't breathe, I can't breathe, I can't breathe . . . I can't breathe."* If you work in philosophy of race and are black or have black ancestry—I am multiracial—and if your personal sensitivity is greater than that of a plant, then the past two years have been painful and shameful to live through. There seems to be something drastically wrong about a justice system that allows police to kill unarmed young black men with impunity, with American elites of all races, who feel sorry for the misfortunes of our already disadvantaged but cannot do anything to help them, with academic whites who have created a discourse about their privilege, and with all those who are apathetic in the face of black tragedy in our time. I wrote this book quickly and with a sense of urgency, in November and December 2014, while interrupting work on a longer and more theoretical project (*Applicative Justice: A Pragmatic Theory for Correcting Injustice*) that will eventually provide more comprehensive underpinnings for this work. In other words, I had to stop philosophizing for a minute, to think about reality.

This book focuses on one specific problem: police killings of unarmed young black men that are not legally punished. The writing also had two specific promptings. First I was inspired by responses to my November 5, 2014 *NYTimes* Stone interview by George Yancy, "What 'White Privilege' Really Means."[1] The liveliest hostile reader commentary (and maybe, also, 1274 'likes' on the *NY Times* Facebook page for November 6[2]) focused on this: *"Not fearing that the police will kill your child for no reason isn't a privilege. It's a right."*

My second inspiration was the heated argument between former New York City Mayor Rudolf Giuliani and Georgetown University Professor Michael Eric Dyson on *Meet the Press* on November 24, 2014. The moderator introduced the claim that white police officers do not racially reflect the population of black communities. Giuliani said it was more important to talk about the fact that 93 percent of blacks who are killed, are killed by other blacks. Dyson said that black-on-black crime was a "false equivalency" to white police officers shooting blacks, because blacks were punished for killing other blacks and white police officers were not. Giuliani said, "White police officers wouldn't be there if you weren't killing each other 70 percent of the time." Dyson replied that Giuliani had a white supremacist mindset.[3]

The same 93 percent figure was trotted out in comments (mostly from Internet 'trolls') about what I said in the *NYTimes* interview. It is completely irrelevant to the discussion of racial profiling and the impunity enjoyed by white police officers who kill blacks in 'stop and frisks' or while attempting to perform stop and frisks.[4] The reason acquittals and failures to indict ignite such strong public protest is that the police are presumed to *protect* members of the communities in which they serve. These ruptures between police and communities undermine trust in government, as well as the constitutional legitimacy of government as represented by such police action and its prosecutorial and juridical blessings. Distrust of government is an unfortunate trend now shared by both extremes of the political spectrum. Tea Party Republicans distrust government because they fear it gives too much to the undeserving. Radicals to the left distrust government because they view it as crushing, when it is not ignoring, the rights of the disadvantaged, especially poor nonwhites, and especially poor blacks. Indeed, a strong case can be made for negative *black male exceptionalism*, not only throughout U.S. history, but in present conditions of police racial profiling and homicide.[5]

Moreover, to bring up the 93 percent statistic when the subject is white police officer homicide following racial profiling is a distraction back to the mode of discourse preferred by those who insist that American society is not racist against blacks. That mode of discourse seeks to find ways to blame victims and hold them responsible for their own misfortune and disadvantage. The reasoning that could be implicit in Giuliani's remarks is that if blacks can be blamed for most of the death rate of young black males, then homicides against blacks committed by white police officers are less blameworthy, by comparison. However, blame is a moral assessment that is not a matter of numbers alone. American citizens have constitutional rights that are at stake in these cases of police homicide. The Fourth Amendment is supposed to protect against arbitrary searches and seizures. The Fourteenth Amendment is supposed to guarantee equal protection under the law and in actions of government officials. Police racial profiling violates both amendments, first by arbitrary stops and searches, and second by disproportionate use of those methods against blacks. The police have a special duty, stated in their oaths, to "uphold the Constitution." That is the issue missed by Giuliani and many others.

Contemporary academic discussion of social justice has now shifted to the discourse of white privilege. I think this is a mistake, insofar as privileges are extra perks and more is at stake in recent police killings of unarmed black men than denial of perks. I hope we have not sunk so low in American society that plain, simple, justice according to the Constitution must be regarded as a perk. Police killings that rest in impunity when grand juries do not indict and trial juries do not convict, violate ultimate, nonnegotiable rights.

About two thirds through the writing of this manuscript, on December 17, 2014, I attended a very timely event at the University of Oregon. Yvette M. Alex-Assensoh, Vice President for Equity and Inclusion, organized "'I Can't Breathe': A Conversation Starter about Racism, Justice, and Love." A diverse group of administrators, staff, faculty, students, community representatives, faith-based representatives, campus police, and city police assembled to discuss the effects on their lives of the recent killings that have not been followed by jury convictions or grand jury indictments, and how a university community might respond.

We sat at round tables of six or eight people, beginning with one-on-one discussions, expanding to full table discussions, and then summarizing to the rest of room. At my table, a young woman of color commented on responses to recent police killings on social media. She reflected that those who were nonwhite among her friends and relations showed engaged responses on their Facebook pages, while her white friends and relations seemed unaware of these events and posted nothing about them. A young white woman at the table talked about the silence on our campus about these incidents. African Americans are under-represented at all levels at the University of Oregon, perhaps reflecting the racial demographics of Oregon itself, which in 2013 had only 2 percent blacks in its population, compared to 13.2 percent for the United States overall.[6] (Oregon's racial statistics may be related to a nineteenth century history of the exclusion of blacks by law, and race-restrictive real estate covenants, which were not fully corrected until 1968.[7])

I was led to wonder if reactions to public trauma depend on the race of those observing and responding. Have we re-inscribed old-fashioned segregation into social media, so that blacks care when terrible things happen to black youth, but whites are unmoved? Is our collective sense of justice dead? I hope not. The great masses of people of all races and ethnicities go about their daily lives, working, socializing, falling in love, ending romantic relationships, raising families, getting sick, and worrying about money. In all of this, most are fully enmeshed in what D. H. Lawrence called the lesser day of ordinary life that can crack "like some great blue bubble" so that we seem to see "through the fissures the deeper blue of that other Greater Day where [moves] the other sun shaking its dark blue wings."[8]

The Greater Day for race in our time is not a matter of what race a person is, but a matter of justice for persons of all races. Justice is not based on common early homo sapiens African ancestry, an immigrant melting pot, or equal opportunities for material success. Justice is a matter of human rights and human dignity. Fortunately, we have a Constitution that names and supports protection for such rights. But unfortunately, that constitution has been interpreted by U.S. Supreme Court judges in ways that ignore both individual and institutional racism. Failure to recognize and support constitutional rights is unjust. People can come together in response to injustice and share the simple, common aspiration that those who are innocent will be left alone by the government as represented by the police and those who are guilty, including the police, will be punished. That aspiration is an attainable goal which we can reach by understanding the nature of the injustices now committed. The focus of this book is very narrow—How do the injustices of the police killing of innocent young African American men work? Why are such homicides not punished? What can be done about this?

In *The Souls of Black Folk*, W. E. B. Du Bois predicted in 1903 that "The problem of the twentieth century is the problem of the color-line—the relation of the darker to the lighter races of men in Asia and Africa, in America and the islands of the sea."[9] More than a century later, it is evident that the color line has blurred in a number of ways: the U.S. Civil Rights Movement has yielded formal equality; the "darker races of men in Asia and Africa . . . and in the islands of the sea" are viewed not in racial terms but in terms of economic development and military capability and threat (which may be as bad, but it is something different); it is well understood by intellectuals in the humanities that much of older definitions of race were based on myths and stereotypes; there is a consensus in the physical biological sciences that racial kinds are not real natural kinds, independently of social divisions that are projected onto genetic and phenotypical taxonomies;[10] in the

United States, where race was most drastically a matter of black and white, multiracial individuals are accorded some recognition and Latino/Hispanics, while officially an ethnicity, nonetheless are regarded as racially nonwhite, for the most part.

However, it is important to return to the black-white dichotomy in these early decades of the twenty-first century, not as a matter of racial identities, but as a matter of justice. Justice, or good enough approximations to justice, exists for white Americans, but not in the same ways for the rest. The starkest examples of injustice are evident in how black Americans are treated by the police. Yes, there is overt and implicit racism and bias, and yes, there are institutional structures, including the U.S. prison system, which make black Americans, especially young males, especially vulnerable. But the crucial issue at stake is application of the forms of justice that are stated in U.S. Constitutional Amendments and the Civil Rights legislation of the 1960s, to black Americans. To do that will require beginning with contemporary instances of race-based injustice that have fallen through the cracks in U.S. Supreme Court Opinions since 1968 and revisiting some of those opinions. This will be a long-term legal project. First, it is necessary to understand how the legal system now works unjustly and how a number of progressive academics, who should know better, have been politically anesthetizing themselves.

Chapter 1 is a critique of white privilege discourse. (It may be experienced as harsh, but I cannot apologize for those effects.) Chapter 2 discusses rights in the context of police racial profiling and attempts a realistic explanation of how and why that practice is unjust. Chapter 3 stresses the importance of beginning with injustice and focusing on its correction, which requires a comparative approach—comparing protection of the rights of whites and blacks. However, because solutions to the present problem are not likely to be found in existing constitutional interpretations and I am not a lawyer, the Conclusion is directed toward solutions that can be crafted within the legal system as it now stands.

I am grateful to my colleague Mark Alfano for reading and commenting on the penultimate draft of this manuscript. Heartfelt thanks to Yvette Alex-Assensoh and her son, Kwadwo Assensoh, for giving that same draft an encouraging reading. I thank George Yancy for long-term ongoing support of my work on race. I am also grateful to Rodney Roberts, José Mendoza, and Janine Jones, for careful readings and comments, only some of which made it into final proofing. Simon Rackham did a great job on the first round of speedy copyediting and Jon La Rochelle did a great job in helping me with final proofs, with exceptional attention to the index. Thanks also to Jon La Rochelle and Sarah Hamid for encouragement during the proofreading stage. I have had support and encouragement from many others, but this book was written too quickly to expect wide feedback in progress. In any case, all of the errors and omissions are mine. Once again, I am very happy to publish with Rowman & Littlefield, and this time I am especially indebted to Natalie Mandziuk for superb editorial performance. Thanks also to Laura Reiter and other members of R&L's production team. All errors and omissions are mine

Naomi Zack
Eugene, Oregon
February 8, 2015

I

WHITE PRIVILEGE, ENTITLEMENTS, AND RIGHTS

Cause of Death: Gunshot wound of the torso with injuries of major vessel, intestines and pelvis.
—Medical examiner Thomas P. Gilson[1]

TAMIR RICE

A video released by the police in Cleveland, Ohio on November 26, 2014, shows Tamir Rice several days earlier. He is aimlessly wandering around in an outdoor recreation center, talking on a cell phone and holding a gun. A bystander called 911 and said that the gun was "probably fake" and that its wielder, although probably a juvenile, was "scaring the shit" out of others nearby. When the patrol car drove up, Timothy Loehmann, twenty-six, a rookie police officer, shot Rice within seconds of getting out of the car. His partner, Officer Frank Garmback, age forty-six, initially remained at the wheel. A report was radioed in: "Shots fired, male down, um, black male, maybe twenty." It was reported that Loehmann and Garmback had not been told that the initial caller reported the gun as "probably fake." We don't know if they had been told that their suspect was probably a juvenile.

Tamir Rice died from his wound the next day. He was a twelve-year-old African-American boy and had been carrying an Airsoft BB gun that officers said resembled a semiautomatic handgun and was without the orange safety marker that would have indicated it was a fake. On the police video, Rice looks like a juvenile, rather than a fully grown adult. The Cleveland NAACP (National Association for the Advancement of Colored People) issued a press statement that reads in part:

> We believe that the ever-increasing tension between the police and the citizens of Cleveland played a significant role in Tamir Rice's death. This shooting brings into question the adequacy of the selection, training and preparation of police officers. Police officers should be prepared to confront and address people of all races and cultures and use deadly force only as a last resort. [2]

Half a century after passage of the U.S. Civil Rights Act, and the formal equality thereby expressed,[3] it has become increasingly popular to address persistent social and institutional racial inequality in a discourse of "white privilege." While whites are undoubtedly disproportionately advantaged compared to nonwhites in contemporary society, much of this discourse remains untroubled by real and raw injustice that is inflicted on black people in the United States. It is not altogether clear what, within the discourse of white privilege, could be said about the shooting of Tamir Rice. If police officers are not "prepared to confront and address people of all races and cultures and use deadly force only as a last resort," the issue is what happens to people that police officers are not prepared to confront and address, on whom deadly force is used according to a standard that is less stringent than a last resort. That is, the issue in this case is how police confront and address black youth and the readiness with which they use deadly force against them. If the police are white, we might say that they have privilege in behaving that way, but not all police officers are white and not all whites are police officers. Perhaps the idea of white privilege applies to those who are not directly affected by lack of preparation of the police to confront and address people of all races and cultures, because they are members of races and cultures who the police are prepared to confront and address and use deadly force against only as a last resort. This seems to be a very roundabout way of addressing an issue of concern to both those engaged in the discourse of white privilege and those who do not have white privilege and do not engage in that discourse.

PRIVILEGE AND WHITE PRIVILEGE

A privilege is something desirable, an extra perk or reward as a result of some prior higher standing or superiority, for example, privileges to use the sauna and tennis courts, enjoyed only by members of the country club. To admit that one has a privilege, even if it is understood that the privilege is undeserved—because one ought not to have the higher standing or is not really superior to those without the privilege—is to implicitly flatter oneself. More seriously, to view oneself as someone without a certain privilege minimizes the importance of what it is that one lacks and creates a situation where one is begging for, or ineffectively demanding, a withheld perk. As a result, those without the privilege and their advocates may be reduced to regarding the "privileged" with envy or blaming them for the condition of those who lack the privilege, while those who admit to having the privilege are often drawn into circles of confession, guilt, and remorse that remain reflective and self-reflective. This is altogether a reduction, not because envy and blame are without grounds or because self-reflective remorse does not strengthen individual character, but because such discourse is a distraction from effective action. However much it has been a good beginning for discussion of ongoing anti-nonwhite racism following the civil rights movement(s), as well as it might afford whites the time and space to psychologically process their individual racism(s),[4] the discourse of white privilege, alone, does not have the gravitas or urgency of either moral principle or social, institutional, and political action. Often (but not always), what is called a "white privilege" that nonwhites lack, is a *right* that is protected for whites and not for nonwhites.[5] That is, a "privilege" whites are said to have is sometimes a right belonging to both whites and nonwhites that is violated when nonwhites are the ones who own it.

If among the comparative advantages whites have compared to nonwhites, rights are not distinguished from privileges, the idea of white privilege easily allows whites who do not have any extra perks to deny that they have white privilege on those grounds, and with that deny the broader concept that includes deep racial inequalities in society. In this chapter, the idea of white privilege is disambiguated by analysis of the foregoing sources of confusion. White privilege discourse is seen to be often misplaced and somewhat insulated from real social injustice, even though its grounding intuition that race-based advantages and disadvantages should be compared, does support social justice.

THE HISTORY OF THE IDEA OF WHITE PRIVILEGE

The idea of white privilege was developed by Ruth Frankenberg and others in the early 1990s, based on statistical and narrative knowledge that whites, because of their race, had advantages in U.S. society that were related to the disadvantages of nonwhites. Progressives had rarely talked about white racial identity before then, partly because whiteness was assumed to be the normal racial identity, so that it did not even seem as though whites had a race. Also, by the 1980s, the long Euro-American history of glorifying the white race had been forgotten and was not at the forefront of general public consciousness. Conservatives who denied racial discrimination and wanted to distance themselves from bigotry had nothing to gain by reminding people of that history and progressives shied away from mention of it, because it was offensively racist.

Only historians and other scholars of race recalled that doctrines of white superiority to nonwhites formed the ideology developed in the late nineteenth and early twentieth centuries to justify Anglo-American Manifest Destiny as the United States expanded "from sea to shining sea," driving out Mexicans and stealing their land, and driving out indigenous Americans and stealing their land. Proclamations of white superiority were also used to justify domination of blacks under Jim Crow laws and the exclusion of Asians in immigration law.[6] Southern and eastern Europeans were admitted during the great wave of early twentieth century immigration, but only because their labor was necessary for an expanding economy. White identity was achieved by Italians, Poles, and Irish Americans, only after several generations of hard work and cultural assimilation. Jews became white only after the horrors of World War II created an association of their nonwhite status with Nazi genocide.[7]

The combination of an ideology of white superiority with such practices of white dominance resulted in a system of white supremacy. It took a while for the declaration of a white racial identity to be possible without invoking or evoking white supremacy. Thus, after the success of the civil rights movements, not much that was positive in an egalitarian or liberatory sense could be accomplished by whites declaring their racial whiteness.

However, by the late 1980s, when it became evident that the United States remained a society of racial inequality, racial whiteness was reexamined, this time not as justification for domination, but to emphasize the role of whites in the unequal system. This new critical identification of whites as a race led to the idea that whites, simply because they were white, had important advantages compared to nonwhites. More than that, some of these advantages were part of a social system that often required no further information about people than their racial identities, in order to dispense such privileges. The disadvantages experienced by people of color were as much, or more, the result of practices and traditions and the ongoing intergenerational effects of poverty and past oppression, as they were the result of prejudice or deliberately discriminatory actions. These enduring practices and traditions constituted ongoing structural or institutional racism.

The idea of structural or institutional racism refers to practices that disadvantage nonwhites in the absence of deliberate racism in the hearts and minds of individuals. Eduardo Bonilla-Silva is often referred to for this concept that can be expanded to all aspects of life. Bonilla-Silva writes:

> There is something akin to a grammar—a racial grammar if you will—that structures cognition, vision, and even feelings on all sort of racial matters. This grammar normalizes the standards of white supremacy as the standards for all sort of social events and transactions. Thus, in the USA one can talk about HBCUs (historically black colleges and universities), but not about HWCUs (historically white colleges and universities) or one can refer to black movies and black TV shows but not label movies and TV shows white when in fact most are. I use a variety of data (e.g., abduction of children, school shootings, etc.) to illustrate how this grammar works and highlight what it helps to accomplish. I conclude that racial grammar is as important as all the visible practices and mechanisms of white supremacy and that we must fight its poisonous effects even if, like smog, we cannot see how it works clearly. [8]

Bonilla-Silva and many other contemporary scholars of race have, as this passage proposes, now moved beyond socioeconomic advantage and disadvantage, to speak of an over-arching system that they call "white supremacy."

IS ANTIBLACK RACISM A WHITE SUPREMACIST SYSTEM?

In 1995, Leonard Harris revealed the steps in a move toward his posit of contemporary white supremacy:

The Ku Klux Klan secretly created a profession: American Philosophy. . . . Once upon a time philosophy, the most honored of intellectual disciplines, joined with American nationalism and the two begot a child: American Philosophy. The new child functioned as evidence for white supremacy because people considered statuses as verification of natures, and consequences were thought to adequately explain antecedents.

Believe It or Not:
        There are no Blacks on the faculty in the Philosophy Department at any of the eight Ivy League universities and no Blacks on the faculty in the Philosophy Department at nine of the eleven Big Ten universities.[9]

The absence or very small number (Harris's stats may have changed a little in twenty years) of blacks at the academic pinnacle of the profession of philosophy can be explained in terms of old-fashioned institutional racism: blacks don't have the same opportunities to pursue philosophy as do whites; the kind of philosophy blacks want to pursue does not meet the needs and wants of Ivy League philosophy departments; some members of Ivy League philosophy departments are not overly concerned with the social justice issue that might be at stake in having a racially integrated profession; some members of Ivy League philosophy departments are antiblack[10] racists in the old-fashioned white-supremacist sense, although they would not explicitly declare that out loud and if it could be proved, the plaintiff in such a lawsuit would win.

        The move toward calling antiblack racist practices a "system" is understandable, given that much of the comparative race-based differences in U.S. life are maintained without individual intent. But is it a *white supremacist* system? After the civil rights movements, overt and deliberate discrimination in education, housing, and employment were made illegal and explicit racially discriminatory laws were prohibited. Whites remain dominant, practices resulting in white advantage continue, and de facto racial discrimination is highly prevalent in desirable forms of education, housing, and employment. However, the absence of an officially-approved ideology of white superiority entails that there is not at present a system of white supremacy. Nevertheless, many contemporary scholars of race call the contemporary United States a "white supremacist society," simply because nonwhites are excluded from so many of the goods of life. That is an exaggeration, because of the present absence of an explicit ideology of white superiority. The use of that exaggeration in the discourse of white privilege may have dire consequences, as will be evident by the end of this chapter.

THE DISCOURSE OF WHITE PRIVILEGE

The discourse of white privilege developed from the realization that whites have racial identities as white and that those identities continue to confer advantages. However, the advantages they confer are the result of institutional and structural racism, as well as lingering prejudice and discrimination on individual levels, and the presence of a small number of explicit white racists who do seek a return to a white supremacist system. Present white advantages are not the result of a white supremacist system and to exaggerate the system of institutional racism or specific racist events, in those terms, is not only a conceptual error, but a political mistake. The exaggeration makes it seem as though the problems that need to be overcome require overcoming a monolithic, overhanging, oppressive political and cultural *thing* that cannot be overcome by nonwhites, because they do not have enough power. Neither can whites be imagined as overcoming white supremacy as posited, because if they were to overcome it, their whiteness, and with that, their dominance, would remain in place. As Steve Martinot puts it, "For white identity to attempt to free itself by rebellion from white supremacy would only reassert a white identity in rebellion and reconstitute the supremacy assumed by its self-definition."[11]

The exaggeration of the problem of racial inequality by white interlocutors in the discourse of white privilege, not only inflates their own importance, but at the same time makes it seem as though nothing effective or constructive can be done to bring about racial equality or even fairness. Thus, Martinot's solution is the familiar self-absorption of his cohort, "a white form of DuBoisian double consciousness . . . that would see itself as those whom whites racialize see it."[12] How does Martinot think that whites can get to know how those whom they racialize as nonwhite see them? Further examination of white privilege discourse will reveal more about its self-paralysis in the face of its stated goals of equality, but first, more distinctions are in order.

WHITE PRIVILEGE AS ENTITLEMENTS

I am not saying that white privilege is not real! Two different kinds of white privilege are at issue here. The first is the easier access whites have to upward socioeconomic mobility and the goods of life available only to the more advantaged in society. The second is the greater likelihood whites have in getting their basic rights protected by government officials and those with power and authority in social institutions, according to the Equal Protection Clause of the Fourteenth Amendment to the U.S. Constitution.[13] Use of the term "white privilege" to refer to both forms of "privilege" equivocates between ideas of entitlements and ideas of rights. Entitlements are advantages for which people are required to perform prior actions to acquire, whereas rights are granted and recognized in virtue of an individual's existence as a human being or membership in a collective (e.g., a community, state, or nation). In a word, privileges are usually conditional, whereas rights are unconditional.

It's easier for whites to attend college, and get advanced degrees that qualify them for management or professional employment. It's also easier for whites to interact with or within the most powerful levels of professional, bureaucratic, and corporate culture, because most of those already there are white. In U.S. society, socioeconomic advance has a strong collegial or social or *cro-*

nyist component, which is easier—and sometimes only possible—to join or navigate if a person is the same race as those
already in positions to which any given upwardly mobile individual
aspires. The same conditions govern election or appointment to
political office. However, degrees in higher education, management or professional employment, and corporate and political
leadership are not rights, but *entitlements*, or in a proper sense of
the word, "privileges." There is nothing frivolous or luxurious
about such "privileges," because they open doors to many of the
material and social goods of life in contemporary society. Still, it
cannot be said that everyone is automatically entitled to occupy
these positions, in virtue of membership in the human species or
citizenship, that is, as a matter of their human rights or political
rights. Furthermore, such entitlements are not privileges attached
to white racial identity, because not all whites have them, particularly poor whites who are greater in number than poor nonwhites
of any one nonwhite (minority) racial group. And, although compared to whites, they are a disproportionately fewer number, nonwhites also have these entitlements.

Entitlements are advantageous positions, some of which are
accorded by merit or the result of hard work, and some as a result
of collegial/social/cronyist patterns of behavior. Still others are
gifts for which a person enjoying them doesn't have to do anything
and doesn't need access to opportunities for inclusion, for example, being born into a rich and powerful family, or inheriting a
fortune, or in Europe, inheriting a royal or noble title.

The disproportionately high possession among whites of desirable entitlements in U.S. society is not in itself the heart of the
inequality that is cause for principled concern. Rather, principled
concern is evoked by who is excluded, based on their racial identities, from entry into realms of advantageous entitlement(s), and
why (when reasons are given for deliberate exclusion), and how
(when social mechanisms result in exclusion) they are excluded. In
our post-civil rights language, such exclusion is described as "lack
of opportunity" or "lack of access." Nonwhites, especially blacks,
were explicitly excluded historically and are indirectly excluded

today. For example, fewer African American children growing up in inner city slums have opportunities to prepare for and apply to colleges than white children growing up in suburbs. The exclusion or lack of access is often the result of unequal distribution between whites and nonwhites of *opportunities*, based on race, socioeconomic position, and race combined with socioeconomic position. Nonwhites, blacks especially, do not have opportunities to acquire these entitlements that are equal to the opportunities whites have to acquire them. That is the heart of the inequality, now loosely referred to by the term "white privilege," and it is what we should mean by "white privilege."

UPWARD MOBILITY, EDUCATION, AND RACE

In dynamic cases of upward mobility, inclusion of members of previously excluded groups amounts to a redistribution of scarce goods. Either some who had easier access lose their points of entry or more points of entry must be created, for example, fewer white students are admitted to the university or university enrollment grows as a direct result of affirmative action or diversity programs. White plaintiffs arguing against "reverse discrimination" have been successful, all the way up through the U.S. Supreme Court, since the late 1970s, based on this presumption and reality of scarcity, i.e., that only so many will be admitted. The Court has ruled that the Civil Rights Act and Fourteenth Amendment of the constitution do not allow "race" to be a positive factor for securing entitlements, even in cases where considering race via affirmative action may be the only way that nonwhites have access to such entitlements.[14] The Court has thereby enacted a very literal understanding of the Civil Rights Act, which prohibited discrimination based on race. Where affirmative action has favored nonwhites who might otherwise experience covert discrimination or who belong to groups still burdened by legacies of past discrimination, the Court looks at "race" only as a property of individuals in the time slice of their application for admission and it rules nonwhite "race" alone, inadmissible to consider. That perspective was explicit in two 2003 cases. In *Graz v. Bollinger*, it was deemed unconstitutional for the University of Michigan to automatically give points for nonwhite racial identity in its undergraduate admissions process.[15] However, in *Grutter v. Bollinger*, it was ruled acceptable for the race of applicants to be considered "holistically," as it was already, in the application process at the University of Michigan School of Law, which showed preference for otherwise competitively qualified nonwhite applicants. Still, the Court expressed reluctance in allowing even this limited consideration of race and Chief Justice Sandra Day O'Connor speculated it would be unnecessary by 2028.[16] Presumably, O'Connor assumed that existing *de jure* equality guaranteed equal opportunity across racial groups, so that it was only a matter of one generation from 2003, when the holistic form of affirmative action would no longer be necessary to achieve *de facto* equality. That is, with one generation of affirmation by race of otherwise qualified freshmen or those seeking advanced degrees, it would no longer be necessary, either for de facto social equality or a recognized desideratum of racial diversity on college campuses, to affirm nonwhite race in the college admissions process.

Upward socioeconomic mobility, by children compared to parents, is a sign of greater opportunities taken by children who rise. In the early twenty-first century, only 35 percent of blacks, compared to 50 percent of whites, exceeded their parents' economic status by more than 20 percentiles. (Upward mobility is highest for white men, followed by white women, black men, and black women.)[17] Upward socioeconomic mobility requires higher education. Grades on standardized tests administered in middle school are a stronger predictor of upward socioeconomic mobility from the status of parents, than any other indicator, including race and gender. Good preparation for standardized tests makes a huge difference, according to a study by Columbia and Harvard University economists, which tracked 2.5 million elementary and middle school students over twenty years. Students whose teachers helped them raise standardized test scores had fewer teenage pregnancies, higher rates of college enrollment, and higher earnings at age twenty-eight.[18]

Compared to whites, poor nonwhites do not have access to higher education without some correctives to their poverty, lack of educational enrichment in K-12, and racial preferences and racist attitudes among both blacks and whites. A poor black child will lack capabilities for higher education because of inadequate teaching, not enough money to attend college, and environmental and external skepticism that she could become a college student. Black families who live in poor neighborhoods send their children to schools with less funding for high quality teachers and educational resources.[19] Black children attending racially integrated schools may encounter bias and stereotyping from teachers, staff, and peers, who are white.[20] Stereotype threat (reminders of minority racial status by a requirement that the test taker identify herself by race) can impair performance on standardized tests, by increasing anxiety.[21] Compared to nonwhites, especially blacks, whites thus have an unearned advantage regarding college admission, which requires even less effort when they are legacy students, whose parents attended any given institution. It seems euphemistic to call this advantage a "white privilege," given the importance of access to higher education for success in adult life. It might be more effective toward "leveling the playing field" to focus on the structural obstacles nonwhites face in a society that valorizes upward socioeconomic mobility in general, instead of dwelling on how whites do not have to contend with such obstacles, as in the present discourse of white privilege. Although, the purpose of white privilege discourse is mainly for those concerned with social justice to develop self-understanding of how society remains racially biased against nonwhites, despite formal equality.

Unequal opportunities for educational entitlements are part of a complex structural condition for all poor families in the United States, consisting of at least these components: less material resources for high quality education in poor neighborhoods; class bias in educational institutions; and lack of motivation due to attitudes from family members and peers in the immediate environment. Remedies would include any and all measures or programs that counterbalance these obstacles. But such remedies are a very hard sell in a political climate that fosters general resentment of any government action to help the poor, especially nonwhites, and especially blacks. Also, as mentioned, affirmative action is all but illegal at the present time. The 1964 Civil Rights Act does support equal opportunity and equal opportunity is generally regarded as a right. Antiracist thinkers generally believe that unequal opportunities constitute rights violations. However, it is difficult to get to rights, including the right of equal educational opportunity, through the discourse of white privilege.

INTROSPECTION AND COMPARTMENTALIZATION

Research in social psychology indicates that if white college students are taught to recognize the "privileges" that are associated with their white racial identity, their resultant guilt may dispose them to discriminate less against nonwhites and actively advocate for social justice on behalf of nonwhites in contexts where they live and work, that is, college campuses.[22] However, while such findings support the importance of education and subjective psychological processing, particularly concerning the "entitlement" aspect of privilege, they do not address more powerful institutional, political, and legal issues. College students who begin with a belief that racial equality has already been achieved in American life and that their greatest problem is "reverse discrimination," are more open-minded than the general population of white Americans who remain skeptical that there is such a thing as white privilege. While it would be a wonderful result of such education, undertaken throughout higher education, if colleges and universities became free of white privilege, there is no guarantee that condition would extend beyond their campuses or that graduates would live out what they learned in college. The mitigation or abolition of both the rights and entitlement forms of what are called "white privilege" may best be supported by such educational and psychological   projects,   undertaken   on   a   subjectivity-targeted "one by one" basis, with the goal of reaching a majority of "ones" in the privileged white population, throughout society. Such educational and psychological projects may even be necessary for abolishing white privilege as both entitlements and rights, but they are not sufficient.

Even if successful, introspective projects do not support a political dimension in white privilege discourse, much less political action toward egalitarian enforcement of rights that already exist. They are also insufficient to generate action that would make institutions and social arrangements more racially egalitarian. A useful comparison here might be with Christianity as a system of beliefs that supports an egalitarian view of humankind and compassion toward those less advantaged than the self. How many white Christian Americans deny both the existence of white privilege and the injustice of institutional racism? How many white Christian Americans would be willing to recognize situations in which their own rights are protected, whereas those of nonwhites are violated? And how many of those white Christian Americans who recognize both white privilege and violation of the rights of nonwhites would be willing to act or support action to correct these inequalities? The point of these questions is not to criticize white Christian Americans but to provide an example of how beliefs, strong convictions even, in one area of life (religion) need not ensue in action in another (politics). White Christian Americans may be likely to ignore white privilege for political reasons, accepted as part of a whole conservative ideological framework that reminds them they have worked hard for their advantages and deserve them. Academics who talk and write about white privilege may similarly hold their progressive belief structures in intellectual parts of their life that are insulated from how they act politically and privately, as well as regarding decisions about dispensing entitlements within the academy.

WHITE PRIVILEGE AND NONWHITE RIGHTS

Concerning rights that are on paper presumed to be "color blind," some writers in the discourse of white privilege believe that a status quo of nonprotection of the rights of nonwhites results in a situation where those whose rights are protected are thereby "privileged."[23] This view regards rights as dependent on whether or not they are enforced, whereas the core of the concept of rights requires that they exist antecedently to their enforcement. Rights are moral conditions of human life that precede law and political action, including law enforcement. Descriptions of rights may be written in declarations and constitutions, but even when they do not have that formal "black letter" expression, rights remain powerful normative aspirations for what the law and its force should protect.

Antiracist scholars are often reluctant to take up the tradition of "rights" as promulgated by the U.S. Constitution and The United Nations Declaration of Human Rights, because such rights have not generally been protected for nonwhites, either within the United States or globally/internationally. However, the discourse of rights is the only existing practical discourse that can lead to the protection of those conditions for human existence that have been called "rights" (they may be referred to by other names, but it is not evident what those may be). Insofar as rights have protection in written law, correction of their violation is in principle accessible through legal action, and the formal successes of the U.S. Civil Rights Movements attest that such action is possible, even though it turns out to be insufficient for achieving antiracist goals, for example, because rulings and laws are not enforced, or because, as already suggested, judicial rulings do not address racial inequalities in society.

Let us now return to inequality of opportunities across racial groups in society, on the presumption that equal opportunities are rights. Conservatives and neo-racists often blame nonwhites for their poverty, under-education, and incarceration. This blame balances a belief that nonwhite races are associated with pathological cultures, on the one hand, and on the other, a belief that as individuals, poor nonwhites have character defects of laziness, lack of self-discipline, and just plain moral badness. Such blame for misfortune and disadvantage could not be propelled toward their targets without an underlying assumption that opportunities are not race-based to the detriment of nonwhites. This is the broad public assumption that "the playing field is level and everyone has the same chance to compete and succeed," together with implicit approval of fairness.[24] That is, the value of fairness is shared by both progressives and conservatives and neo-racists.

American citizens have a constitutional right to vote, which is a political opportunity. The Voting Rights Act of 1965 was meant to protect the rights of blacks to vote in southern states and localities where white officials obstructed that right, by providing for federal judicial jurisdiction over "voting qualifications or prerequisites." The 113th Congress passed the Voting Rights Amendment Act of 2014, stating that it "Expands the types of violations triggering the authority of a court to retain such jurisdiction to include certain violations of the Act as well as violations of any federal voting rights law that prohibits discrimination on the basis of race, color, or membership in a language minority group." However, the act also "Excludes from the list of violations triggering jurisdiction retention authority any voting qualification or prerequisite which results in a denial or abridgement of the right to vote that is based on the imposition of a requirement that an individual provide a photo identification as a condition of receiving a ballot for voting in a federal, state, or local election."[25] As of this writing, a number of states are in the process of passing, or have passed, voter photo identification requirements, and a debate is in process: proponents claim that the measures are necessary as protection against voter fraud; opponents claim that the risk of voter fraud has been exaggerated, photo identification requirements make it more difficult for some poor, nonwhite, and elderly citizens to vote—and that the requirements favor Republicans, because those voters without photo IDs are more likely to vote for Democratic candidates.[26] No one can credibly say that nonwhite citizens do not have a right to vote. But if photo ID requirements for voters result in fewer nonwhites voting, because of that requirement, alone, the effect will be to turn a right into an entitlement, by making the unconditional right to vote subject to unequal, race-based abilities to perform.

More extreme putative rights violations are at issue in cases of antiblack racial profiling by police, particularly when confrontations escalate into the killing of unarmed suspects. The sense that rights have been violated intensifies when police who kill in such instances fail to be criminally indicted or are acquitted in criminal trials for manslaughter or murder. It was presumed to be in anticipation of such failure to indict that the U.S. Human Rights Network organized a trip to Geneva, Switzerland, for the parents of Michael Brown to speak before the United Nations Committee Against Torture, in November 2014, following Brown's killing in August.[27] The perception of injustice has expanded after the grand jury's decision not to indict police officer Darren Wilson, who fatally shot him. Events such as this spark impassioned expression, physical demonstrations and protests, spikes in local gun sales, and stronger law and order capabilities from local authorities. They also cry out for analyses in terms of rights and justice.

WHITE PRIVILEGE, RESPONSIBILITY, AND MANNERS

The discourse of white privilege, as an academic discourse, is not generally structured around arguments or claims concerning human rights that extend to nonwhites, which could be enforced in concrete ways. Rather, this white privilege discourse is isolated and stalled in its lack of robust ideas of white responsibility. What, again, is white privilege according to this discourse? The answer is that compared to how whites are treated, nonwhites are routinely treated unjustly, cruelly, and unfairly. The discourse of white privilege succeeds when white people recognize this fact. But along the way toward that white epiphany, white privilege is often discussed as though it is an impersonal, thoroughly institutional system of direct rewards for white people, because they are white, whereas rewards are withheld from nonwhite people, because they are not white. The result is that the location of the white interlocutor in the very system she is required to recognize and criticize, is neglected. At the same time, there is insufficient focus on any responsibility that a white-privilege interlocutor may have, for "white privilege" as a system, and, more importantly, no attention is paid to action she can take to mitigate or abolish this system.

The system referred to in "white privilege" discourse distributes or dispenses privileges to whites, which are not so much directly withheld from nonwhites (many of whom remain unaware of the extent and complexity of "white privilege"), as simply not available to them. This was done directly in the past, solely based on racial identity, e.g., only whites could vote, marry other whites, use certain bathrooms, enroll in most colleges, etc. Today, the privileges referred to as "white privileges" are often distributed or dispensed indirectly, so that merit, education, wealth, experience, beauty, or certain traits of character, as well as certain social relations, are required in order to get entitlements to varied goods of life. But the indirect system remarkably mirrors the prior direct system. White people end up getting a disproportionate share of the rewards and goods of life. They don't get as large a share as whites in the past got, but there is a disproportion, nonetheless. White participants in the discourse of white privilege apprehend such persistent inequality, but without fully apprehending their own place in the system.

The system of white privilege is dominated by white people. White people hold the majority of its political offices, control most major corporations, fund or run most institutions of higher education, and so forth. And "rank and file" whites act in ways that preserve this structure, in their private, public, and social lives. *This means that white people distribute and dispense privileges to other white people that they do not distribute and dispense to nonwhite people.* What the white interlocutors in the discourse of white privilege often fail to acknowledge is that as white people they themselves dispense what they are identifying as "privileges," to other white people. Barbara Applebaum puts this very well: "The emphasis on personal awareness . . . overshadows the need for understanding and challenging the system of power that supports white privilege."[28] If white people want to do something to mitigate or abolish the injustice of white privilege, they could stop distributing and dispensing these privileges to other white people, in their own lives. That would be the active response to what has been given to them with no effort, for example, Peggy McIntosh's list of valuable items in the famous invisible backpack (sometimes called a "knapsack") of white privilege.[29] Furthermore, it is important to recognize that what Applebaum calls "the system of power that supports white privilege" is itself the system of white privilege.

In practical terms, intervening when white privilege is dispensed is likely to come down to changes in the accessibility of entitlements that are not available to nonwhites. Within schools, corporations, and other practical institutions, it may not be whites alone who dispense privileges to whites and exclude nonwhites, so that instead of overt and identifiable privileges dispensed only by whites, it may be that nonwhites are implicitly or covertly or inadvertently overlooked for opportunities that are in principle "race blind." Here, "white privilege" is a matter of institutional racism or bias and those who are aware of their white privilege may not have an obligation to divest themselves of that privilege or the entitlements it has made possible. But they do have an obligation to make the institution in question more egalitarian. While working to change an institutional practice in a school or corporation is not quite the same thing as directly doing something positive as a white individual with power and authority that nonwhites do not have, it is certainly worthwhile. Still, the kinds of actions white privilege interlocutors feel empowered to take as individuals, are more likely to be matters of manners than "institutional politics."

Failure to put themselves in the picture of the white privilege they decry can render white interlocutors in the discourse of white privilege, apolitical, passive beneficiaries of a system they fail to imagine changing. As a result, in its more confessional moments, the discourse flails as a kind of anguished "meta" view from nowhere. As Alison Bailey put it in 1999, "I can't divest myself fully of privilege, and its use only fortifies the system I want to demolish. I can't lose it and I don't want to use it. Where do I go from here?" Bailey goes on to relate her direct assistance of a black student who was receiving racially discriminatory treatment from the payroll office in her university (a check was being withheld and racist stereotypes were invoked as a justification) as an example of a positive use of the resources of white privilege.[30] In a volume appearing in 2015, Marilyn Nissim-Sabat in "Revisioning 'White Privilege'" gives an account of a going-away party, where she was the only white person present, a tense situation that she dispelled by announcing her knowledge that all whites, as well as blacks, have distant ancestors in Africa.[31] In another 2015 volume, Nancy McHugh agonizes over her racism of twenty years earlier, when in a car with white friends she referred to black families enjoying a Baltimore evening outside their homes, as "porch monkeys."[32]

The examples in these essays show that white privilege discourse is not exactly about how people of color experience racism or about how white people who believe that their privilege is morally wrong should behave toward people of color, but about the grace required from whites who recognize the system. Bailey and Nissim-Sabat recognize that because they are white, they have a certain power in real events in their daily lives. And, as both a remedy to their white privilege, which also uses it, each author relates having done something ameliorative for specific nonwhites, Bailey to counter antiblack discrimination and Nissim-Sabat to reassure blacks (it is not clear about what). Each is a good act in its context, motivated by good intentions. Bailey performs a courtesy for her black student in helping her get her check and Nissim-Sabat is socially polite in finding something to say that puts others at ease. McHugh's self-castigation is about an insult that its objects did not even directly experience. (But is it likely that the black people she referred to as "porch monkeys" did not already know that some whites called them that, and worse?)

Still, we do need to consider the rudeness toward American blacks that is accepted in the routines of American life, and to appreciate the importance of manners in race relations. President Barack Obama referred to antiblack racial suspicion among whites, several days after George Zimmerman's acquittal in the criminal trial for his killing of unarmed Trayvon Martin[33]:

> There are very few African-American men in this country who haven't had the experience of being followed when they were shopping in a department store. That includes me. There are probably very few African-American men who haven't had the experience of walking across the street and hearing the locks click on the doors of cars. That happens to me—at least before I was a senator. There are very few African-Americans who haven't had the experience of getting on an elevator and a woman clutching her purse nervously and holding her breath until she had a chance to get off. That happens often.[34]

George Yancy used the same examples of car doors clicking and a white woman clutching her purse in an elevator, as reactions to his presence as a black male, in *Black Bodies/White Gazes*, which was published in 2008.[35] (The coincidence of the President using the same language and the same examples may show how common such experiences are in twenty-first-century America, that his speechwriters practice plagiarism, or both.)

African American males are discriminated against in the examples described by Yancy and Obama, in a unique way. They are not explicitly excluded or devalued, but instead receive special, heightened attention, because they are believed to pose dangers that nonblacks do not pose. Simply, their racial identity or their racial identity combined with male gender, counts as evidence of wrong doing, without any evidence of criminal intent, much less criminal action. Yancy writes, "It is as if my black body has always already committed a criminal deed."[36] This kind of discrimination and stereotyping by whites apparently requires no justification.

Awareness of a black male presence is allowed to automatically evoke, not only fear, but defensive precautions (locking car doors, clutching purses). Quite apart from often violent developments, such rudeness by whites toward blacks immediately conveys a bad first impression, based on race and gender alone. When the victim is innocent of any wrongful intent, as is more often than not the case, that black male victim will have experienced a very deep insult, an acting out of shunning, through extreme social rudeness that only whites have the privilege and authority to express with impunity.

Courtesy and politeness are essential social virtues and they lubricate hierarchical social systems by creating an atmosphere of respect for those with lower status and less power, in this case, respect for nonwhites as generic human beings and/or even as those with lower status. However, such respect for nonwhites by whites in a society that is deeply structured to maintain historical disadvantages of nonwhites, especially blacks, is superficial and meretricious. It does nothing to disturb white privilege as a social and institutional system. The racist "system" may be understood and white individuals may even "get it," which is to say, recognize that it is racist and thereby unjust. But insofar as nothing in reality is imagined as *systematically* changing as a result of that realization and no action is taken against that system, it could be said that the white interlocutors in the discourse of white privilege succeed in becoming subjects when it is a matter of reflection and verbal sharing, but fail to become subjects in planning and acting justly, their politeness notwithstanding. This is not a failure to "change the system," which is impossible for an individual to do, but an *akrásia* or failure of action by an individual, on the assumption that there is something she could and should do, but is not doing. Of course, shame at such inaction could become another confessional subject, but if/when that happens, the discourse of white privilege, as undertaken by white subjects in an anti-nonwhite racist society, becomes a self-indulgent end in itself. The discourse of white privilege can thereby become no more than an exercise of white privilege, something new and fresh in its self-reflexivity, but old and toxic in its reproduction of racial inequalities. This discourse of white privilege has now entered philosophy via narratives or narratives combined with critical analysis, written mainly by white women, who are often also feminists. Their personal accounts do challenge arid, artificial rigor in the style of our discipline, but rarely go beyond displaying the suffering and discomfort of women who are privileged in the context of their suffering and discomfort. And they may not even suffer! For instance, in talking about white New Wave and No Wave music, Robin James relates:

> I, a white girl from the Midwest, like this music. I find it pleasurable not only because I hear anti-racist and often feminist and queer politics in it but primarily because I like the way it sounds. I like its awkwardness, its herky-jerky, jaggedy, irregular, contorted aesthetic. Maybe it reflects my own dis-orientation, the epistemic and affective noise I feel in my complex inhabitance of whiteness and contradictory relationship to white hegemony. If being white means participating in and benefiting from white privilege, then I am, in some ways, on the one hand, condemned to be and do things that disgust me. On the other, less flattering hand, I may appreciate at some level, privileges that I intellectually know are immoral and unjust.[37]

WHITE PRIVILEGE AND SHAME

Shame over white privilege may be self-indulgent even without personal disclosure or confession. For instance, the emblematic and social-political aspect of Trayvon Martin's death has raised existential questions for whites, who recognize responsibility for the role of their racial "groups" in constructing a system in which unarmed young black men may be summarily killed by police or auxiliary law enforcement personnel. In "Politics, Moral Identity and the Limits of White Silence," Samantha Vice, a South African philosopher, discusses the potential offensiveness to blacks if whites express solidarity or speak out uninvited against the injustice of such cases. Vice concludes that while a white person's universal moral identity may prompt spontaneous declarations in such situations, silence may be a better choice because it will avoid what blacks might perceive as arrogant and intrusive. Vice opines: "Whatever the reasons that this death, out of many others, has been taken up as a public political event, whites are restricted by decency in what we can now say, even out of sympathy and solidarity."[38] According to Vice, then, white shame when blacks are treated unjustly should result in respectful *silence* on the part of whites. It's not altogether clear why this should be the case.

Silence, no matter how morally agonizing to those holding their tongues, is easier than speech or action. How does Vice know——for surely it's an empirical matter—how the families of young unarmed black men who have been killed in such circumstances would react to uninvited white consolation? The public does not lack for racist white commemorations of such events, such as the successful sale in Florida of gun targets with a silhouette meant to depict Trayvon Martin.[39] Would it indeed be unwelcome and disrespectful if white members of a Chamber of Commerce in a locale where an unarmed black teenager was killed made it a practice to issue a declaration of outrage? Michael Brown's father told a CNN reporter that he had received no word of condolence or apology from the Ferguson Police Department, between the time of the shooting of his son and the release of the grand jury decision not to indict Officer Wilson. He said he considered the silence "cruel and unfair . . . no handshake, no hug, no nothing."[40] Would expressions of sympathy to the family sent by the local chapter of the Daughters of the American Revolution indeed constitute an unwelcome intrusion? What if more "left-leaning" but overwhelmingly white organizations, the American Philosophical Association, for example, issued supportive and sympathetic statements in cases like this? It is generally understood, in the United States at least, that invitations are not required for sympathetic people to show up at funerals, and the public expressions of grief that follows these events are virtual funerals.

Silent shame is not inevitable. Although white participants in the discourse of white privilege cannot as individuals change the whole system, they can act to correct or stop themselves and other whites from dispensing primarily to whites, entitlements short of rights. This can, and indeed has already, led to policy changes within institutions and corporations regarding entitlements that had been dispensed mainly to whites. It has also changed what is "PC" (politically correct) in polite, educated society. Such change includes understanding and support by whites of court and legislative action, when the protection of rights is at stake. And it requires and has called forth considerable commitment to thinking as clearly and rationally as possible about how the rights of non-whites continue to be violated in our post-civil rights era. Why that is unjust will be the topic of chapters 2 and 3. To complete this discussion of white privilege discourse, it is important to consider how it can lead to despair and may set the stage for violence.

WHITE PRIVILEGE DISCOURSE, VIOLENCE, AND DESPAIR

Physical violence is directly destructive action. There is no evidence that violence for the cause of black men who are automatically criminalized could change the causes of that criminalization. Over the twentieth century and into the present one, there have been many places in the world where violence resulted only in death, human harm, and collateral human harm. The police in the United States now have military equipment and if they cannot stem violence from civilians, it's a short step to real military presence with state National Guard units and should that fail, federal troops. Nobody wants that and it is unlikely to end well. Yet, violent reaction and counter-action to police impunity in the arbitrary killing of black men is on a lot of people's minds. Gun sales after the St. Louis Grand Jury's refusal to indict Officer Darren Wilson for the killing of Michael Brown on November 22, 2014, spiked during the weekend following that Thanksgiving. For Black

Friday alone, the FBI reported over 175,000 "checks," compared to 58,000 for a typical day in 2013.[41] News outlets as far away from Ferguson, Missouri as New York City reported that this spike in gun sales was a reaction to the protests in Ferguson. While it should be noted that the biggest gun sale day on record occurred a week after the Sandy Hook school massacre on December 21, 2012, which was not a racial event, the connection between the 2014 spike in gun sales and the Ferguson protests is about racial injustice. We don't know the race of those who bought the guns, of course, but immediately after Michael Brown was killed, spikes in gun sales for "home defense" were reported and no black concerns about home invasion were reported.[42] In other words, violent protest by blacks or fear of it probably increases armed preparation among some whites.

Violence on the part of blacks and their supporters to arbitrary police violence is not only a bad thing in itself, but is likely to be self-defeating. And yet, in the context of speaking from the context of white privilege, in a *NYTimes* interview in The Stone, Shannon Sullivan recently raised the specter of violence:

> The potential for racial conflagration is very real, I think, even beyond what we recently have seen in Ferguson. Would it be effective in changing the institutional, national, global and personal habits that need to be changed to take down white supremacy? I worry that violence is a shortcut that doesn't help remake habits, racial or otherwise, and so it won't solve the long-term problem. At the same time, you and I should be suspicious of that worry. It's very convenient, isn't it, for a white person to have philosophical reservations about the effectiveness of violent black resistance?[43]

Shannon implies that blacks will commit the violent actions. That leaves her safe as a nonviolent white philosopher who is worried about both the violence and her own worry about it.

Hope is more than a general attitude because usually we hope for something specific to happen. When hope for a specific change is dashed, the specter of despair arises.[44] For many years, black

Americans and their supporters have rhetorically sought to "keep hope alive" (Reverend Jesse Jackson has a radio show by that name[45]). The implication is that this is hope for justice, equality, and an end to arbitrary white violence against blacks. Keeping hope alive in the sense of general optimism is simply good sense and good mental health. But hoping for specific outcomes without knowing how to work toward their reality or what such work would require, can be a form of passivity, as in the difference between wishing and willing. So maybe hope is an attitude that needs to be expressed by intentions to bring about specific ends.

In the aftermath of the St. Louis Grand Jury verdict on the death of Michael Brown, placards began appearing with the words, "Black Lives Matter." This was reminiscent of Kanye West's reaction to the slow federal response to the plight of black victims after Hurricane Katrina: "George Bush doesn't care about black people."[46] Shannon Sullivan in the same interview mentioned earlier, wrote: "America is fundamentally shaped by white domination, and as such it does not care about the lives of black people, period. It never has, it doesn't now, and it makes me wonder about whether it ever will."[47]

"BLACK LIVES MATTER"

What does it mean to say that black lives do not matter in America? It's not a claim that can be taken literally. Black people clearly did matter to George Bush, as voters and those who could make the moral judgment that he was a racist (which he denied).[48] All of the famous cases of the deaths of unarmed black men and boys by U.S. police were mourned by their families and protested by sympathizers. Obviously, the lives taken mattered to those who lost them. To say that America does not care about the lives of black people means that in the moments of confrontation, everything happens as though the risk of death to a black male was not the most important consideration to police officers who fired. And it means that grand juries who did not indict such killers, or juries who found them not-guilty at trial, found that other things mattered more, such as, the letter of the law, police discretion and relative police autonomy, and reasonable doubt.

What it credibly means to say that black lives do not matter in America is that compared to white lives, they are not treated with the same respect and concern and there are not comparable efforts taken to preserve and protect black lives. That is not the same thing as black lives not mattering, although it is a situation that calls for justice. Before we can talk about justice, more needs to be understood about the specific injustices that keep recurring. We need to understand how such perceived injustices follow actions that are perfectly legal in a nation with a strong Bill of Rights. Relevant laws and court decisions should be able to shed light on why such injustice is not punished, in a legal system that, on a state by state basis, imprisons more people than anywhere else in the world.[49] Chapter 2 will contribute to that understanding by taking a close legal and moral look at several specific cases and the police racial profiling that sets the stage for both such arbitrary violence and its impunity.

2

BLACK RIGHTS AND POLICE RACIAL PROFILING

No one should live in fear of being stopped whenever he leaves his home to go about the activities of daily life.
—U.S. District Court Judge Shira Scheindlin[1]

BLACK RIGHTS, CIVIL RIGHTS, AND HUMAN RIGHTS

What are black rights? There are no distinctive rights that people have based on race and to combine a racial adjective with the word "rights" is a rhetorical device. Still, with true premises, a persuasive argument about black rights can be framed:

1. As human beings or American citizens, blacks and whites have the same rights.
2. Blacks have been deprived of rights compared to whites who are not so deprived.
3. It is unjust that blacks are deprived of rights whites have.
4. To bring attention to this injustice and encourage respect and protection of the rights of blacks, so that blacks are not disproportionately deprived of rights, it is useful to talk about "black rights."

The 1960s Civil Rights movement was about the violation of rights that African Americans already legally had, such as rights to integrated education and voting rights. To bring attention to the reality of the violation of blacks' legal rights, it was effective to think and talk about "civil rights," which meant practices of recognition and protection of the legal rights of African Americans. The rhetorical move was not unique. The United Nations first framed its Universal Declaration of Human Rights (UDHR) in terms of universal human rights, in 1948. But the UN has since found it necessary to issue numerous proclamations and declarations about the rights of many groups of humans whose human rights are consistently violated: racial minorities, refugees, women, children, disabled people, indigenous people, the poor, and so forth.[2] Thus, in speaking of black rights, the real subject is violation of the rights of blacks, which are also the rights of whites. (There may also be a subtext that the rights of blacks are violated, because they are black.)[3]

IDEAL RIGHTS AND MATERIAL RIGHTS

It is useful to distinguish between *ideal rights* and *material rights*. Ideal rights are abstract, whereas material rights pertain to physical conditions and how existing human beings are treated, primarily regarding their most basic bodily rights to life and safety. Declarations of general or specific rights by the United Nations are mainly ideal, because there is no world government or police force, with the aim and ability to protect those whose human rights are violated. In the United States, by contrast, there are both stated rights of citizens and residents, or ideal rights, and, because there are both state and federal governments, it is expected that such rights not only refer to material conditions, but that they will be materially, that is, physically, protected. Concerns about rights discourse usually focus on the ineffectiveness of ideal rights alone. But where there are material rights matching them, in a structure of practices by government officials, ideal rights have a material counterpart.

In the United States, the majority of white citizens and residents have both ideal and material rights. The first level of rights protection, material rights to life and personal security, is largely carried out by members of local police departments throughout the country, as part of their official duties. We need to take a look at how that occurs, in the context of police culture, before proceeding with this discussion of rights.

COMMITMENTS OF U.S. POLICE OFFICERS

American police are expected to take "The Police Officer's Oath," that varies slightly by locale, in accord with the following:

> I, *Name*, do swear that I will well and truly serve our sovereign country and state as a police officer, without favor or affection, malice or ill-will until I am legally discharged, that I will see and cause our community's peace to be kept and preserved and that I will prevent to the best of my power all offenses against that peace and that while I continue to be a police officer I will to the best of my skill and knowledge discharge all the duties thereof faithfully, according to law. So help me God. [4]

In addition, The International Association of Police Chiefs has endorsed an "Oath of Honor":

> On my honor, I will never betray my badge, my integrity, my character, or the public trust. I will always have the courage to hold myself and others accountable for our actions. I will always uphold the constitution, my community, and the agency I serve. [5]

These police oaths state general intentions and commitments in an abstract or ideal way, but they lack rules of application, or guidelines for specific physical cases. Such guidelines can be inferred from customary practice, court decisions, and the extent to which police departments are influenced by public opinion, all of which vary. There is little evidence, however, that actual police policies are directly *derived* from the U.S. or State Constitutions. To "uphold the constitution" is a vague and metaphorical term. In reality, actual practices are tailored to the prevention of crime and the apprehension of criminals, as police deem effective.

Police leaders may be appointed or elected,[6] which determines to whom they will be accountable in their normal course of discharging duties. It seems as though election would be more democratic in matters of race, than appointment, in requiring that police represent community members they serve. But, communities are not racially monolithic and elected police chiefs could in reality be accountable to only dominant racial groups in the community. Appointed police chiefs in racially conservative police departments could be accountable to progressive local government officials. In principle, the actions of all police officers make them accountable, after the fact, to judges and juries, internal police department review processes, and perhaps also, reactions from the public that are protected by the First Amendment.

The U.S. police force is racially integrated, but in hundreds of departments, particularly in the Midwest, the proportion of white officers is more than 30 percent higher than the proportion of whites in the communities they serve. About one quarter of all police are nonwhite.[7] It would be inaccurate to say that American police are overwhelmingly white. But the main part of their job is to apprehend criminals and the culture and attitude of American police officers inevitably reflect who they think criminals are. And they seem to strongly associate nonwhiteness, especially blackness, with criminality.

HOW CRIMINALS ARE DEFINED

If police believe that most criminals in an area are nonwhite or that nonwhites are more likely to be criminals than whites, then their perspective may be biased in favor of whites and against nonwhites, in the process of carrying out their law enforcement duties. Indeed, one way to define a criminal group, which has evolved as a preferred American definition, is by rates of incarceration among different racial groups and/or the racial makeup of the prison population. These are not the same numbers, and they are complicated by whether they are taken for any given year, or over a period of years, due to recidivism. In the United States, of 2.2 million people in jails and prisons in 2005, 900,000 were African American. The Bureau of Justice Statistics reports that from 2001 to 2005, African American males were incarcerated at 5.6 times the rate for white American males.[8] Antiracist academics usually approach these figures as symptomatic of a social problem, but many members of the civilian public take them as straightforward evidence of *who* American criminals are. There is little reason to believe that American police do not read such figures in the same way as those members of the civilian public.

Police oaths are suitable for public display and exhibition to white middle class school children. White school children from middle class families generally have no reason to be skeptical about such displays and good reason to trust the police, because the police are there to protect them. The poor of all races, and blacks, especially, are taught by their family members and peers that their lives and safety depend on understanding that they do not have good reason to trust the police. Why?

THE REASON IS NOT WHITE SUPREMACY

Let's discount as an explanation that the United States is a white supremacist society and that the police enforce the basic principles of white supremacy. For one thing, such an explanation is tautological, both based on evidence such as police behavior toward nonwhites and used to explain that evidence. And apart from that, white supremacy now has a stable meaning throughout the culture. From the standpoint of most, if not close to all American police officers, avowed white supremacists pose their own dangers, because they are armed and generally anti-government in all its forms. (Although this is not to be able to say that avowed white supremacists are not members of some U.S. police departments.[9])

In interpreting recent, past, and ongoing shootings of unarmed young black men by police officers, it could be said that *everything happens as though the U.S. were a white supremacist society and that the police enforce its basic principles.* But to put it even in that qualified, hypothetical way (i.e., as what philosophers would call a transcendental argument) is imprecise. And precision is important here, because the practical correction of the injustices involved in police racial profiling and police homicides against unarmed black men will lie in addressing certain details. I claimed in chapter 1 that the United States is not at this time a white supremacist society, because it does not have an official ideology of the superiority of the white race and there are no laws explicitly preferring whites or exclusionary or punitive of nonwhites, simply on the grounds of race. This is not to say that implicit or privately-held explicit beliefs about white superiority are not prevalent, but that if persons, especially government officials, act based on those beliefs, they have to be able to justify their action by producing reasons that do not invoke their beliefs about white superiority.

One practical reason for claiming that the U.S. is not at this time a white supremacist society is that legal remedies for specific instances of presumed white supremacy on the part of the police are usually sought by families of victims, who are not white. These nonwhite families hope and work for criminal indictments and jury verdicts of guilt against the officers who have killed their sons. They prosecute wrongful death lawsuits against municipalities that are the employers of police officers who have killed their sons. Videos of police killings of unarmed black men circulate on the Internet, and documentaries and special television programs are produced about them. None of the foregoing actions and events would or could be undertaken in a white supremacist society, not even one that cherished its First Amendment and other constitutional rights. Moreover, police killings of unarmed black men spark widespread rage and public demonstrations, as well as serious discussion by people of all races.

HOW APPARENT RACIAL BIAS IN POLICE WORK WORKS

So how does it work? How, if the United States in the twenty-first century is not a white supremacist society, do American police both take and publicize such oaths, while at the same time, practice what appears to be racial profiling with now known and widely publicized devastating consequences? First, the oaths assert loyalty to country, state, and "badge" or local department—not to everyone in the communities where they serve. Second, it is in the context of oath taking, at official ceremonies, that "accountability and responsibility" are mentioned—the police are accountable and responsible to those to whom they swear their oaths. Second, concerning content, in the "Policeman's Oath," the importance of preserving peace is emphasized, but there is no mention of justice. Third, the oaths make no mention of fairness, or the protection of rights, or an absence of specifically racial bias. The oaths support a view that those who obey the law have nothing to fear from the police, who will preserve peace, presumably by apprehending or taking other action against those who are a threat to peace. To generally keep the peace for the law-abiding, and keep them safe, is a tall order. To carry it out, police need rules of thumb, ways of distinguishing between people who are likely to be lawful, who they can largely ignore, and those likely to commit crimes, on whom it is their job to focus.

There is a broad underlying presumption throughout American society and probably police culture, also, that some people need to be protected against other people, and police departments are generally focused on protecting that group or class which is respectable, employed, has low crime conviction rates, and is more or less the same race as the police. Blacks and latinos are disproportionately sentenced for crimes in the United States, compared to whites. ("Sentenced," rather than convicted, because the number of felony cases that go to trial is now less than 5 percent.[10,11]) The NAACP Criminal Justice Factsheet states: About 14 million Whites and 2.6 million African Americans report using an illicit drug. Five times as many Whites are using drugs as African Americans, yet African Americans are sent to prison for drug offenses at ten times the rate of Whites.[12]

American police officers are given no reason to believe, as part of their official assignments or duties, that there is anything unjust about racially disproportionate sentencing.[13] It is not the job of uniformed police officers to critically examine the justice of the U.S. Criminal Justice System. That the same actions, for example, recreational drug use, are prosecuted as crimes when committed by poor nonwhites, but overlooked when middle class whites commit them, is not a surprising set of statistics for police officers and their leaders, because they are not concerned with groups already determined to be mostly law abiding. Instead, their focus is on members of groups known to produce a high rate of sentenceable and sentenced crime. American police officers and administrators are not antiracist theorists or social workers in search of the causes of disproportionate crime rates as related to race.

American police officers and administrators come into the whole crime-race scenario *after* the race-related facts of incarceration have been established, and their general charge is to act on the basis of those facts. Such action may, in academic antiracist speak, "reinscribe" the problem of the association of nonwhite race with incarceration, but that is not the practical problem for police officers carrying out their duties. (Although, it may be a problem for higher level police administrators, who are persuaded to address it by public protests, and criticism by concerned members of the public, the academy, and perhaps the federal government.[14])

Police officers have individual discretion about when and how to use force to fulfil their duties, and to assess the degree of force necessary in immediate situations. The independent nature of patrol jobs entails that officers are not under constant supervision through the chain of command in their departments. The rationale for police discretion is that their jobs, especially if they are in uniform, are universally believed to be high risk for their own lives and personal safety. (Death on the job for police officers was 19 per 100,000, ranking the occupation tenth most dangerous. Fishing and fishery workers have the most dangerous job with a death rate of 116 per 100,000.[15]) Stress and stress-related illness are additional factors.[16]

While American police officers are undoubtedly taught key aspects of the U.S. and relevant state constitutions as part of their classroom training, they are not lawyers and it is not their job as police officers to interpret or enforce constitutional rights, in the course of their duties. It is therefore misdirected to look to uniformed police officers as agents of antiracist change, even though they are "the law" for all practical purposes. Still, that a scattered, but ideologically-united army of uniformed (as well as uninformed) young men are the law throughout the United States, is cause for serious concern. Legitimate limitations in the scope of crime detection and prevention duties may be compounded by individual differences in character, attitude, and competence. For example, Tim Loehmann, the rookie police officer who killed Tamir Rice, within seconds of jumping out of his car where the twelve-year-old suspect was playing with a fake (toy) pistol, had received negative evaluations during his firearms training, two years earlier. The Deputy Chief of the Independence, Ohio Police Department reported that during his firearms training, Loehmann was "distracted" and "weepy" and "did not appear mentally prepared" for the task. This report on Loehmann continued:

> He could not follow simple directions, could not communicate clear thoughts nor recollections, and his handgun performance was dismal. Unfortunately in law enforcement there are times when instructions need be followed to the letter, and I am under the impression Ptl. Loehmann, under certain circumstances, will not react in the way instructed.[17]

Loehmann was asked to leave the Independence Police Department, but he then enrolled in and graduated from the Cleveland Police Academy. When the Cleveland Police Department hired him, apparently no one looked at his earlier record.[18]

RIGHTS AND LAW

We need to return more critically to the subject of rights. What are rights? I've already written in chapter 1: "Rights are moral conditions of human life that precede law and political action, including law enforcement. Descriptions of rights may be written in declarations and constitutions, but even when they do not have that formal 'black letter' expression, rights remain powerful normative aspirations for what the law and its force should protect." However, rights discourse is inherently vague. Usually (as I did), someone refers to rights to emphasize a strong belief, typically about what others are not allowed to do to a person or, more controversially, what a person is entitled to. For example, insofar as others are not allowed to kill me, I have a right to my life that is violated if someone kills me without good reason, such as their self-defense. And there are other qualifications. To violate my right to my life, they must kill me deliberately, and there has to be prior agreement on what good reasons are (so we can tell if they are absent). If I die in a war, my right to life has probably not been violated and I may jeopardize my right to my life by engaging in a violent crime or attacking someone else. At the beginning of this chapter, distinctions were made between ideal rights, which are aspirational only, and material rights that refer to physical conditions of existence. I suggested that material rights exist in the United States, where individual rights are explicitly stated in foundational documents and there are government capabilities to protect them.

However, the combination of documented rights and government capabilities to protect them does not mean that they will automatically be protected. Does a right still exist if it is violated?

Can the right be claimed in the face of its continual violation? The answer to each question is Yes, provided we do not *expect* automatic and immediate material expression from the combination of ideal expression and material government capability. Thus, there are ideal rights and material rights and material rights have two parts—physical capabilities to protect ideal rights and actions to protect ideal rights or the exercise of relevant material government capability.

Why should everyone have the same rights? Answers to that question have ranged from religious foundations to narrow legal contexts, with no universal agreement, and that has resulted in frustration with rights discourse. The Universal Declaration of Human Rights (UDHR) says in its preamble that we are all members of the same "human family," with inherent "dignity" from that same membership: "Whereas recognition of the inherent dignity and of the equal and inalienable rights of all members of the human family is the foundation of freedom, justice and peace in the world." [19] This wording implies the existence of some underlying human equality, but it is virtually impossible to find a common ground for human rights in equal human abilities or needs. Humans are deformed for good or ill by their immediate physical and cultural environments from the moment of birth, and that alone makes them sufficiently unequal to support any doctrine of equal rights.[20] Human needs can be defined in basic biological terms, for example, food and shelter, but they vary greatly. Also, persistent global starvation and problems of homelessness in rich societies have not generated solutions based on rights discourse, because human needs, as rights, are positive entitlements, requiring generosity and widespread agreement to recognize and meet. UDHR lists a number of such entitlements as rights, including minimum incomes, but such positive rights do not have material expression in U.S. law or political and social practice.[21]

The UN's reference to "inherent dignity" could be based on human subjectivity or self-awareness and life interests, but not all humans have these, or even the potential for them, and many animals, whose rights are not widely recognized, do have both self-awareness and interests. Still, the idea of universal human rights remains inspiring and it is worthwhile to look for an empirical basis for it, even if the basis is not universal or inclusive at the outset.

RIGHTS DISCOURSE, INDIVIDUALS, AND GROUPS

As vague as rights discourse generally is, some precision can be found in specific rights under the political jurisdiction of a government that is obligated to uphold such rights, for instance, the Bill of Rights or first Ten Amendments to the U.S. Constitution. However, as noted, there is no guarantee that even such political or *civil rights* will in reality be recognized for members of all groups in the United States. (Lack of recognition undermines their ideal status and lack of protection blocks their material expression.) African American citizens do not in reality enjoy the same rights and protections as white Americans. Furthermore, insofar as the language of the written law does not recognize racial groups but pertains to individuals, it is difficult to make discrimination against groups a cogent and compelling legal issue. The Fourteenth Amendment, the 1964 Civil Rights Act, the 1965 Voting Rights Act, and the 1965 Immigration and Nationality Act, prohibit discrimination against individuals on the grounds of race, religion, creed, and so forth, but do not prohibit discrimination against groups. The Fourteenth Amendment reads in part, "No state shall make or enforce any law which shall abridge the privileges or immunities of citizens of the United States; nor shall any state deprive any person of life, liberty, or property, without due process of law; nor deny to any person within its jurisdiction the equal protection of the laws;"[22] The Civil Rights Act reads in part, " in determining whether any individual is qualified . . . to vote;"[23] The Voting Rights Act reads, "No voting qualification or prerequisite to voting, or standard, practice, or procedure shall be imposed . . . to deny or abridge the right of any citizen of the United States to vote, on account of race or color;"[24] The Immigration and Nation-

ality Act refers to persons, "No person shall . . . receive any preference or priority or be discriminated against in the issuance of an
immigrant visa."[25]

By contrast, in the Fourth Amendment, there is a general reference to "the people," which reads:

> The right of the people to be secure in their persons, houses,
> papers, and effects, against unreasonable searches and sei-
> zures, shall not be violated, and no warrants shall issue, but
> upon probable cause, supported by oath or affirmation, and
> particularly describing the place to be searched, and the per-
> sons or things to be seized.[26]

It seems reasonable to speculate that if the people have a right to
be secure in their persons, and if an identifiable group of the
people, such as young black males, is insecure, that their Fourth
Amendment rights have been violated. Seemingly arbitrary stop
and frisk procedures would seem to be "unreasonable searches";
Police homicides following stops and frisks, or attempts at them
are considered "seizures."

Before the civil rights legislation of the 1960s, there was overt
discrimination against groups, for example, "No Blacks," "No Col-
oreds," and "White Only" appeared on public signs.[27] However,
the laws against individual discrimination seem to leave group discrimination undisturbed and prejudgment of groups, or prejudice,
is not illegal. The persistent use of racial stereotypes entails that in
people's minds, the treatment of individuals may be mediated by
beliefs about the racial groups to which any individual is presumed
to belong. But, so long as stereotypical beliefs about the racial
group are not expressed or explicitly tied to the treatment of the
individual, discrimination is not illegal. Reasons other than stereotypical thinking can almost always be found and used as rational-
izations or alibis for discriminatory behavior. American law does
not regulate what goes on in people's minds regarding racial
groups, and indeed would protect whatever that may be, as a First
Amendment right. Still, in an age of almost complete surveillance

and recording of private speech, when racist thoughts about groups are voiced by officials or others in prominent public positions, repercussions can be swift. For example, Los Angele Clippers' Owner, Donald Sterling, was expelled by the NBA for recordings of conversations in which he told his girlfriend not to bring her black friends to games.[28]

In police racial profiling, racial discrimination against an individual may be mediated by named and observed "behaviors" more prevalent in one racial group than another, and such behaviors may be invoked as a justification for a practice of racial profiling. If the named "behaviors" are real and are culturally associated with nonwhite racial identities, at a given time, then police racial profiling is another form of structural racism, analogous to environmental racism. Americans are legally allowed to be prejudiced against racial groups and such prejudice as motivation for discriminatory treatment of individuals can easily be masked by other reasons for discriminatory behavior.

HATE CRIMES

The legal focus on individuals makes it difficult to match race-based patterns of discrimination in reality, or group discrimination, with what is written in statute, case, and constitutional law, in order to identify a group-related rights violation. And even if a pattern of such violation is established, in the United States, there are no laws against discrimination against whole groups, except for hate crimes, which are very narrowly defined. The FBI, based on definitions provided by Congress, defines hate crimes as follows:

> A hate crime is a traditional offense like murder, arson, or vandalism with an added element of bias. For the purposes of collecting statistics, Congress has defined a hate crime as a "criminal offense against a person or property motivated in whole or in part by an offender's bias against a race, religion, disability, ethnic origin or sexual orientation." Hate itself is not

a crime—and the FBI is mindful of protecting freedom of speech and other civil liberties. [29]

Notice that it is not a crime in the United States to hate a racial group. First Amendment rights protecting free speech can block the legal prosecution of hate speech, Other countries have different policies regarding hate speech. For example, according to CBC News, Canada, "Under Section 13 of the Canadian Human Rights Act it is a 'discriminatory practice' to send hate messages via telecommunications equipment, including the Internet."[30] In the United States, according to the legal definition of a hate crime, racial bias, or hatred together with violent action, may not constitute a hate crime. To be guilty of a hate crime, the offender must commit a criminal act that is at least partly motivated by hatred of the minority group to which the victim belongs. The motivation referred to here is not a general disposition that an agent may have, but a specific motive for the specific act. Thus, someone who hated black people and killed a black person because he or she suspected that black person of wrongdoing, would not necessarily be charged with, or if charged, found guilty of, a hate crime—the killer could be motivated by fear in the immediate situation.

Except for egregious acts of racial violence that are explicitly motivated by racial hatred alone, hate crimes, as legally defined—that is, the criminal act is, when committed, at least partly motivated by hatred of the victim's minority identity—are relatively rare in the United States. For 2011, the FBI reported 4,623 hate crime offenses, classified as crimes against persons, of which 19.4 percent were aggravated assaults and only four were murders—out of a total of 12,668 murders. [31,32] Thus, racial bias as an attitude in individuals, a practice of racial bias, as in racial profiling, and a chain of events that culminate in a white police officer killing an unarmed black suspect, do not add up to a hate crime.

Discrimination against an entire group is not precluded by U.S. anti-discrimination laws, and when it underlies behavior toward a particular individual, it is very difficult to prove. Often, when the treatment of two racial groups are compared, some legitimate or justifiable concern of those who discriminate mediates what has the effect of group-based discrimination. For instance, environmental racism, or dumping toxic waste products in poor, nonwhite neighborhoods, has been defended by corporations on the grounds that they are not discriminating by race, but seeking cheap real estate for their refuse, where residents lack power to sue them.[33] While economic class discrimination and bullying are morally reprehensible reasons, they are not direct forms of racial discrimination. Corporations may be telling the truth in claiming that they are motivated by economics and power, and unaware of the consequences of actions in nonwhite neighborhoods, where residents and their advocates experience the dumping as a form of racism. Still, there is more explicit awareness of race in police racial profiling.

POLICE RACIAL PROFILING

Most of the well-publicized cases of police killings of unarmed young black men have two distinct phases, followed by two distinct reactions to perceived injustice. First, there is racial profiling and a "stop" or an attempt to make a stop. That situation is followed by the application of lethal force in the homicide cases. The public then responds to the death of an unarmed black man. After a passage of time, when such protests have abated, there is a trial or grand jury investigation. Typically, the police officer is acquitted of a crime or not charged with one and that decision is followed by additional public protest. Police racial profiling thus enables the use of lethal force—lethal force has been used in attempts to stop and frisk and in confrontations during stop and frisk (as well as in other contexts, of course.) Lethal force, as perceived to be unjust, is distinct from the failure of the law to punish police officers for killings related to stop and frisk activities. Police racial profiling thereby needs to be considered separately from the issue of legal responsibility for the death of its subjects.

Racial profiling is a crime prevention and detection method used by police officers, which takes racial identity into account to select and investigate suspects. There is a drastic view of this strategy, according to which some nonminority police officers actively hate and seek to harm members of minority groups, which motivates them to hunt them out for invasive and oppressive treatment, misusing and abusing their own authority in the process. This would be racist racial profiling, which for the sake of discussion, I will assume (hope?) can be addressed through official police channels. What we should consider, as a failure of the application of U.S. Constitutional rights, is a form of racial profiling that is considered legitimate, and is presently legal.

In a text presented by the National Criminal Justice Reference Service, as part of the U.S. Department of Justice's Office of Justice Programs, Darin D. Fredrickson and Raymond P. Siljander claim that it is important to distinguish between criminal profiling and racial profiling. They write in their abstract that "criminal profiling" is "crime detection wherein police officers are perceptive to various indicators suggesting that someone may be engaged in criminal activity." They state further that "a criminal profile will often include, among other things, race and/or national origin, or some other protected category," and that it should not be confused with "racial profiling," which is discriminatory and, according to the authors, in violation of either Fourth Amendment or Fourteenth Amendment rights.[34] How can the race of suspects be legally relevant to crime detection? If witnesses have already identified a suspect by race, then race may be used for identity in a neutral way. But bias may be part of the process if police rely on crime statistics to identify suspects. Racial minorities, particularly blacks and Hispanics, disproportionately make up the U.S. prison population. And in any given area or neighborhood, those caught and convicted of certain types of crimes may disproportionately be members of minority groups. So, in a crude way, the discriminatory form of police profiling might be justified on the basis that the probability that a random black male is a criminal is higher than the probability that a random white male is a criminal.[35] Or, it may be that in a certain neighborhood or region, most crimes of a specific type are committed by members of a distinct racial group. As discussed earlier, it is not part of police procedure to question the justice of the U.S. criminal justice system. Nonetheless, if it is unjust that nonwhites are disproportionately incarcerated, then reasoning that results in racial profiling based on race and incarceration alone, is indirectly unjust.

The New York Civil Liberties Union claims that 90 percent of those detained by stop and frisk practices by police have been completely innocent. Since 2002, there have been over 5 million street interrogations and stops conducted by the New York Police Department (NYPD). Between 2012 and 2014, 50 to 55 percent of those stopped were black, about 30 percent were Hispanic/ Latino, and 10 to 12 percent were white.[36] Over the same time period, the black and Hispanic/Latino populations of New York City were 25.5 and 28.6 percent of the population, and whites 33.3 percent.[37] Blacks appear to be five times as likely to be stopped and frisked as whites and they are only a quarter of the population, while whites are a third. Within the 2010 national prison population, 380 whites per hundred thousand were incarcerated, compared to 2,207 blacks.[38] The black rate of incarceration is about 5.8 times the white rate and the black rate of stops are about 5 times the white rate. Is there a formula for stop and frisk, internal to the New York City police department, that tracks the national incarceration statistics?

FLOYD V. THE CITY OF NEW YORK

Is it correct to consider racial profiling in terms of rates of incarceration? It is correct if rates of incarceration are just, but if they are unjust, then it could be unjust to relate the two as a matter of police procedure. Similar reasoning related to the NYPD's use of racial profiling appeared in the Opinion of U.S. District Court Judge Shira A. Scheindlin in the contentious 2013 case, *Floyd v.*

The City of New York. In her Executive Summary, citing previous court decisions, Scheindlin wrote:

> The Supreme Court has held that the Fourth Amendment permits the police to stop and briefly detain a person for investigative purposes if the officer has a reasonable suspicion supported by articulable facts that criminal activity "may be afoot," even if the officer lacks probable cause. Reasonable suspicion is an objective standard; hence, the subjective intentions or motives of the officer making the stop are irrelevant. The test for whether a stop has taken place in the context of a police encounter is whether a reasonable person would have felt free to terminate the encounter. To proceed from a stop to a frisk, the police officer must reasonably suspect that the person stopped is armed and dangerous.
>
> The Equal Protection Clause of the Fourteenth Amendment guarantees to every person the equal protection of the laws. It prohibits intentional discrimination based on race. Intentional discrimination can be proved in several ways, two of which are relevant here. A plaintiff can show: (1) that a facially neutral law or policy has been applied in an intentionally discriminatory manner; or (2) that a law or policy expressly classifies persons on the basis of race, and that the classification does not survive strict scrutiny [i.e., where the legislature has passed a law to further a compelling government interest and has narrowly tailored the law to achieve that interest[39]]. Because there is rarely direct proof of discriminatory intent, circumstantial evidence of such intent is permitted. The impact of the official action—whether it bears more heavily on one race than another—may provide an important starting point.[40]

Scheindlin noted that the factual evidence suggested that the number of stops were likely higher than the NYPD database reported for 2004 to 2012, because officers did not always submit paperwork. She found the reasons for stops—usually "Furtive Movements," "High Crime Area," or "Suspicious Bulge"—subjective and vague. At least 200,000 of the reported 4.4 million stops for that period were (conservatively) found to be unjustified based on those criteria. At any rate, only 6 percent of the 4.4 million stops over the period resulted in arrests. On the basis of Fourteenth Amendment requirements of equal protection by government officials, regardless of race, Scheindlin rejected the claim made by the City's experts that "the race of crime suspects in the area of stops is the appropriate benchmark for measuring racial bias in stops." Her reasoning was that most of those stopped were innocent. She accepted the plaintiff's suggestion that a better measure for police deployment than the one in place would be a combination of local demographics and local crime rates. The difference between the NYPD's practice and Scheindlin's recommended method is this: NYPD —In a black neighborhood, most crimes would be committed by blacks, permitting NYPD to practice random stops, according to their current practice; Scheindlin's Recommendation—In the same black neighborhood, stops would not be random but would require a degree of probable cause, to bring the stop rate closer to the actual crime rate in that neighborhood.

Because the plaintiffs in *Floyd v. The City of New York* requested an injunction against the NYPD and Scheindlin did not have the power to request a jury (to decide on the facts), she had to both decide on the facts and apply relevant legal principles. These were her main findings on the facts: The NYPD carries out more stops where there are more black and Hispanic residents; The stop rate exceeds the crime rates in these areas; blacks and Hispanics are more likely than whites to be stopped in even low crime areas; blacks were 30 percent more likely than whites to be arrested following a stop for the same crime and force was 14 percent more likely to be used on blacks than whites; however, the likelihood that a stop would result in further law enforcement action was 8 percent lower for blacks; and, the greater the black population in a precinct, the less likely that a stop would result in further law enforcement action. Scheindlin concluded, "Together, these results show that blacks are likely targeted for stops based on a lesser degree of objectively founded suspicion than whites" [in violation of the Equal Protection Clause of the Fourteenth Amendment].[41]

In 1999 the New York State Attorney General had placed the City of New York on notice that its stops were conducted in a "racially skewed" manner. Despite that notice, NYPD officers were subsequently pressured by their supervisors to increase the number of stops they made. Stops increased from 314,000 in 2004 to a high of 686,000 in 2011. NYPD had a policy of targeting "the right people" for stops, which meant young black and Hispanic men. Scheindlin stated that this use of race was a form of racial profiling, which violated the Fourteenth Amendment by placing all members of a racial group under criminal suspicion, because some members were criminals. Scheindlin further found that the City of New York was liable for violations of the plaintiffs' Fourth and Fourteenth constitutional rights, because it was "deliberately indifferent" to the NYPD's actions in conducting unconstitutional stops and unconstitutional frisks.

Scheindlin ordered several remedies including: immediate change in "certain policies and activities of the NYPD"; a trial program of body cameras for police officers; a community-based joint remedial process conducted by a court-appointed facilitator; appointment of an independent monitor to ensure that the NYPD's conduct of stops and frisks is "carried out in accordance with the Constitution and the principles enunciated in [her] Opin-ion, and to monitor the NYPD's compliance with the ordered remedies."[42] However, before these remedies could be enacted, Scheindlin was recused from the case by a three-judge panel from the U.S. Court of Appeals for the Second Circuit, on the grounds that she was not impartial and had violated the judicial code of conduct. Corporate Counsel on behalf of the City requested that all of Scheindlin's remedies be vacated. The Appellate panel re-jected this request and the City appealed that. Meanwhile, NYPD's stop and frisk activities continued.[43] All of this court activ-ity occurred during the administration of New York City Mayor Michael Bloomberg (2002-2014).

THE BROKEN WINDOW THEORY

It should be emphasized that Scheindlin made it very clear at the outset of her Opinion that she was not ruling on the effectiveness of NYPD's stop and frisk policies. Had she examined whether crime rates decreased over the period, the defense would probably have presented expert claims about the Broken Window Theory, introduced by James Q. Wilson and George Kelling, in 1982.[44] Wilson and Kelling proposed that enforcing public order in neighborhoods might be a neglected tool for preventing more serious crime, both as a rational deterrence and for building pride and care about local communities among residents. Wilson and Kelling's reference to minor offenses, such as drinking in public, loitering, and disorderly conduct, seem to be more extreme than the "Furtive Movements, High Crime Area, or Suspicious Bulge," reported by the NYPD as reasons for stops. Also, it has not been confirmed that procedures based on Wilson and Kelling's theory, which had been put into practice in New York, Chicago, and Los Angeles by the early 2000s, were effective in reducing more serious crime. Crime, especially violent crime, decreased by 48 percent from 1993-2011, a trend that began before stop and frisk policies were adopted.[45] And finally, the Broken Window Theory has not been confirmed. Re-examination of a 2001 study by George Kelling and William Sousa about crime data from 1989-1998 in New York City has not supported a direct correlation between public disorder and crime.[46]

Before taking office, Bill de Blasio, New York City Mayor Bloomberg's successor (De Blasio is a Democrat, Bloomberg a Republican), said he would withdraw the City's appeal of the Appellate Court's refusal to vacate Scheindlin's Opinion. In October 2014, de Blasio's withdrawal of the City's appeal was granted, thereby lifting the hold on Judge Scheindlin's remedies, which had been put in place one year previously.[47] The NYPD has not been happy with that turn of events and on December 13, 2014, New York City's largest police union, the Patrolmen's Benevolent Association (PBA) posted the following notice on its website:

DON'T LET THEM INSULT YOUR SACRIFICE! Download and sign a request that Mayor de Blasio and City Council Speaker Melissa Mark-Viverito stay away from your funeral in the event that you are killed in the line of duty. Completed forms may be given to your PBA delegate.

PBA President Patrick Lynch said that in supporting protests against the grand jury decision not to indict Officer Daniel Pantaleo for the chokehold that killed Eric Garner, de Blasio had "thrown [cops] under the bus," adding, in reference to de Blasio:

> He spoke about, "we have to teach our children that their interaction with the police and that they should be afraid of New York City police officers." That's not true. We have to teach our children, our sons and our daughters, no matter what they look like, to respect New York City police officers, teach them to comply with New York City police officers even if they think it's unjust. [48]

It is not clear from this how Lynch's idea of respect for NYPD officers, consisting of called-for compliance, together with a belief that what one is complying with is unjust, differs from fear.

NATIONAL AND INTERNATIONAL RACIAL PROFILING

In contrast to his attempts to implement Scheindlin's recommendations, de Blasio has been accused, in several pending lawsuits, of maintaining the Bloomberg Administration policy of spying on suspected Muslim terrorists, via a religious/racial profiling program directed at that community. [49] American-style police racial profiling now has a global dimension, as well as the U.S. nationwide local one, in the ongoing War on Terror. [50]

On December 8, 2014, the Obama Administration limited federal racial profiling within the United States, but not for airport screening or border checkpoints. Under the new guidelines, race can be taken into account by federal law enforcement, only if it is known beforehand that race is relevant to who committed a crime. Federal law enforcement officials cannot blanket entire groups in search of suspects.[51] However, the new federal guidelines are not binding on local police and it is well known that if a crime was committed by a black man, the result is often arbitrary stops of all and any black men in an area, or that a claim that a black was known to commit a crime can easily be used as an excuse for stopping black individuals. It is therefore difficult to see how these new federal guidelines would have any effect on current police practices.

The End Racial Profiling Act of 2013 (S.1013-113th Congress 2013-14) has been introduced in both the U.S. House of Representatives and Senate. It "requires federal law enforcement agencies to maintain adequate policies and procedures to eliminate racial profiling and to cease existing practices that permit racial profiling." On December 9, 2014, hearings were held on the bill in the Senate by the Committee on the Judiciary Subcommittee on the Constitution, Civil Rights and Human Rights.[52]

Scheindlin's Opinion, the dependence of its legal practicality on local politics, remaining police racial profiling, and the intense reactions of police against restrictions on racial profiling, indicate that in reality, racial profiling cannot be easily eradicated in New York City at this time. And there is little reason to believe that antiracist judges and public officials will be able to quickly prevail over police departments in other parts of the United States. It therefore remains important to develop conceptual framings of the main issue involved, which can steer clear of both hearts-and-minds racism (protected by the First Amendment) and local power plays and their attached rhetoric.

THE ABUSE OF STATISTICS IN RACIAL PROFILING

It is not realistic, as a proposed solution to similarity between racial profiling statistics and incarceration racial statistics, to demand or expect that police will inform themselves about the racial injustice of the criminal justice system. They should, but that would be asking too much of the white, conservative-inflected, culture within U.S. police departments. Perhaps what is needed is a different kind of argument, a "reframing" of the problem that moves it away from what does or does not count as racism. Considering the entire U.S. population, here are the double-edged figures, used by progressives to emphasize race-based disadvantage and by conservatives to justify racial profiling: 1 in every 15 African American men and 1 in every 36 Hispanic men are incarcerated in comparison to 1 in every 106 white men.[53] What is overlooked in this picture is that these figures entail that most African American and Hispanic men, like most white men, *do not* commit the kinds of crimes for which police seek suspects. The problem with both racial profiling by police and the reasoning of those who defend it, is a focus on the racial makeup of the criminal population. What this focus leaves out is the majority of people in minority groups, who are law-abiding, but are nonetheless, because of their nonwhite appearance (especially if it is black) more likely than whites to be suspected of crimes. If 14 out of 15 or more than 93 percent of African American men are not "in" the criminal justice system, compared to more than 97 percent of Hispanic men and 99 percent of white men, then racial profiling that relies on the racial proportions of convicted criminals ignores the rights of the overwhelming majority who are law-abiding—in all races.

It is unifying that progressives and conservatives use the same statistics in their approaches to crime! Conservatives believe that those in the criminal justice system deserve to be there, especially nonwhites who disproportionately make up criminal populations. Progressives believe that the disproportionate numbers of incarcerated nonwhites reflect the depths of race-based disadvantage in American society. Some incarcerated nonwhites do not deserve to be classified as criminals, because they are in prison only because they have been singled out by police profiling, which was followed by other racial biases in the legal system. In these arguments, both sides miss the fact that the overwhelming majority of American men, more than 90 percent, are not criminals. Not coincidentally, when 4.4 million random stop and frisks were conducted in New York City, during the period from 2004-2012, even though blacks were disproportionately singled out, the incidence of further police action was less for blacks than for whites.[54]

Out of respect for the noncriminal majority, it should be remembered that the rationale behind due process procedures is to protect those who are innocent. In that law-abiding context, racial profiling, which takes into account only the racial identities of those men convicted of crimes, who are altogether a small numerical minority of the total population of American men, is unjust. Racial profiling is unjust, because it *arbitrarily* targets members of a law-abiding, numerical majority, at any given time. It is indeed, as Judge Scheindlin wrote, (quoting Charles Blow), like "burning down a house to rid it of mice."[55] And given the dangerous force routinely at the discretion of police, when racial profiling goes bad, before an innocent suspect can establish his innocence, the results may be tragic.

Consider the Trayvon Martin case in this regard. George Zimmerman, an armed neighborhood watch captain, took it upon himself to track Trayvon Martin, an unarmed black seventeen-year-old, returning home in a gated community. They had a confrontation and Zimmerman shot and killed Martin.[56] When the probability that Martin was a criminal is properly assessed at under 10 percent, Zimmerman was not justified in assuming that Martin was a criminal or, if he was, that he was in the process of committing a crime at that time (criminals do not commit crimes all the time).

Of course, crime statistics refer to entire populations and if they are applied as probabilities to numbers smaller than an entire population, there is no guarantee that the smaller number is representative. Some police officers might assume, given the total statistics, that if there are fifteen black males before them and fifteen white males, it is more likely that one of the black males is a criminal, than one of the white males. But the sample is rarely that small and if racial profiling is practiced over a large city, there is reason to believe that the targeted population is representative. As noted, there were 4.4 million stop and frisks in New York City from 2002-2012, and half of the subjects were black. Overall, 2.2 million blacks were stopped by the police and 90 percent or close to 2 million were innocent. That is a lot of innocent people!

THE RIGHTS OF THE INNOCENT

It is reasonable that the police would be more interested in who is criminally guilty than who is innocent, because that is their job. But for society more broadly, the well-being of the innocent is more important. Not only do the innocent not deserve invasive suspicion, but they are the numerical majority. There is an interesting moral choice, here: Which is preferable, to punish more guilty people if the only way to do that involves punishing some innocent people, or to allow all or most innocent people to remain unpunished if the only way to do that results in some guilty people remaining unpunished? Something like this dilemma occurs in arguments for and against capital punishment, because a system of capital punishment, while carrying out ultimate consequences for the worst deeds, will inevitably result in death for some falsely convicted innocents. But there is a huge practical difference, because the number of those who are innocent of what police suspected in stop and frisks are readily available (all those let go without further police action), while innocence after conviction in capital cases requires painstaking proof.

Precedent for the idea that it's more important to save innocents than punish the guilty is found in Genesis:

> And Abraham drew near and said, Wilt thou also destroy the righteous with the wicked? Peradventure there be fifty righteous within the city: wilt thou also destroy and not spare the place for the fifty righteous that are therein? . . . And the Lord said, If I find in Sodom fifty righteous within the city, then I

will spare all the place for their sakes. And Abraham answered
and said, . . . Peradventure there shall lack five of the fifty
righteous: wilt thou destroy all the city for lack of five? And he
said, If I find there forty and five, I will not destroy it. And he
spake unto him yet again, and said, Peradventure there shall be
forty found there. And he said, I will not do it for forty's sake.
And he said unto him, Oh let not the Lord be angry, and I will
speak: Peradventure there shall thirty be found there. And he
said, I will not do it, if I find thirty there. And he said, Behold
now, I have taken upon me to speak unto the Lord: Peradventure there shall be twenty found there. And he said, I will not
destroy it for twenty's sake. And he said, Oh let not the Lord be
angry, and I will speak yet but this once: Peradventure ten shall
be found there. And he said, I will not destroy it for ten's sake.
(*Genesis* 18:23-32)

William Blackstone took up the biblical injunction in the context
of British law: "Better that ten guilty persons escape than that one
innocent suffer."[57] The principle of sparing the innocent has a
long anecdotal history in law and letters, but at certain times in
U.S. society, it has been replaced with blame and vengeance and a
lack of charity toward suspects or possible suspects. Still, there is
more than kindness toward the guilty at stake in protecting the
innocent. It is the innocent for whom the idea of rights works
best—Fourth Amendment rights, rights to be left alone, rights to
probable cause before police act on their suspicions, and many
other preconditions for well-being in society. The American system presumes innocence, with guilt requiring proof—"innocent
until proven guilty." Police racial profiling leaves such rights undisturbed for whites, but only because they are not profiled as
criminal suspects. If innocence or guilt cannot be separated from
ideas of race by law enforcement officials, and guilt is uniformly
associated with nonwhite race, then indeed, in that context, there
is a white supremacist system, because innocence is explicitly
superior to criminality and whites are explicitly believed more
likely to be innocent and blacks more likely to be guilty. But notice
that these explicit projections of guilt and innocence that may

motivate individual police officers who practice racial profiling, arise only in the context of considering the entire population of innocent and guilty, white, and nonwhite. The uninformed reasoning from racial statistics in the prison population to (as a basis for) police racial profiling becomes white supremacist when applied to a whole population of whites and nonwhites.

THE PSYCHOLOGICAL EFFECTS OF RACIAL PROFILING

There are many publications in philosophy of race and throughout the humanities about the interruptions to innocent well-being from the experience of even routine and relatively mild police stops that follow from racial profiling. The 2014 American Philosophical Association Committee on Public Philosophy's Op-Ed prizewinning essay was George Yancy's "Walking While Black in the White Gaze," that first appeared in The Stone, *NYTimes*.[58] Yancy relates a traumatic moment of danger in an encounter with a white policeman:

> "Man, I almost blew you away!"
> Those were the terrifying words of a white police officer—one of those who policed black bodies in low income areas in North Philadelphia in the late 1970s—who caught sight of me carrying the new telescope my mother had just purchased for me.
> "I thought you had a weapon," he said.
> The words made me tremble and pause; I felt the sort of bodily stress and deep existential anguish that no teenager should have to endure.

A recent study of the effects of stop and frisk encounters was based on a telephone survey of 1,261 young men aged 18-26. Respondents reported intense reactions, including risks to mental health, such as heightened anxiety resulting from repeated "stops." [59] When the courts have decided against stop and frisk policies, their invasive and aggressive nature has been acknowledged by judges, for example, "It is simply fantastic to urge that [a frisk] performed in public by a policeman while the citizen stands helpless, perhaps facing a wall with his hands raised, is a 'petty indignity.'"[60]

It is important for police officers to understand the effects of their attitudes on young minority males, because the tone of long-term police-resident relationships are likely to affect short-term incidents. Rod Brunson and Jody Miller's 1999-2000 study of forty African-American men, ages thirteen to nineteen, living in St. Louis, Missouri, was reported with a review of relevant literature. All forty subjects of the study were classified as "at risk," according to social service agencies; 65 percent had been arrested at some time and 50 percent had been arrested in the previous year. The young males in the study had frequent experience with proactive police stops, while walking or driving. Based on in-depth interviews and survey questions, 83 percent reported "harassment" by police and 93 percent said they knew someone else who had been harassed—these numbers included half of those who had never been involved in any serious delinquent activities. Subjects reported random stops, sometimes while walking to school, which involved rude language, shoving, hitting, being knocked to the ground, and ordered to take their clothes off in winter weather.[61] Brunson and Miller drew the following conclusions: Aggressive behavior on the part of police during encounters is directly related to the degree of noncompliance on the part of someone stopped. But, if police behavior is regulated, male members of minority groups are more likely than whites to comply with police requests. Residents of poor minority communities, blacks especially, experience disproportionate amounts and degrees of police surveillance, disrespect, and physical force. Minority distrust and dissatisfaction with police in their community can be directly traced to such negative experiences with police.

While the majority of young men in Brunson and Miller's study had some kind of "record," the surveillance to which police constantly subjected them, together with rude and physically aggressive behavior in stops and frisks, meant that the police presumed constant guilt of crime and behaved accordingly, with the added factor of personal disrespect. Police behavior toward this group not only failed to follow due process, but showed little regard for the rights of those who were innocent. In addition to the ongoing operation of a self-fulfilling prophecy about young black male criminality, perceptions of the police in this study read more like reactions of residents under siege by a hostile occupying army, than members of a community interacting with those sworn to preserve peace. The overall implication of such situations is that U.S. police engaged in proactive crime prevention need to be given accessible opportunities to see themselves in action, as others see them.

BODY CAMERAS?

Perhaps, in an electronic society such as ours, a requirement that all police on duty wear body cameras with constant "selfie" functions is a good idea. However, body cameras should not be viewed as a panacea. Howard Wasserman cautions that any such solution proposed in moments of "moral panic" is likely to be disappointing. Studies of the use of body cameras by police do report fewer stops and frisks and greater forbearance. But what gets recorded is never completely without bias and the same can be said for how it is subsequently interpreted.[62] Also, when there has been video evidence of brutality or homicide by police, it has not precluded acquittals at trial, for instance in the Rodney King case, or more recently Officer Johannes Mehserle's trial for killing Oscar Juliuss Grant III,[63] as well as recordings of the chokehold that killed Eric Garner. As long as racial profiling is an accepted and legal policy, and police have discretion in what counts as legitimate force when carrying out that policy, a record of ensuing events will not address either the policy or the discretion. What is urgently needed are practical procedures that interrupt events leading to police homicide against unarmed subjects and long-term changes in the law.

But first, it is important to further understand how the present
system with its recent high profile casualties *is* within the law.

3

BLACK INJUSTICE AND POLICE HOMICIDE

If somebody shoots somebody else, the medical examiner's going to call it a homicide. Now whether it's criminal, is a different story.

—Lawrence Kobilinsky[1]

COMPARATIVE INJUSTICE

The subject that rivets the attention of everyone in the discourse of white privilege, as well as anti-racist thinkers who might have reservations about that discourse, rests on an answer to this question: Are blacks in the United States treated justly in comparison to whites? If the answer is No, which I am provisionally going to assume it is, then the discourse of white privilege shifts to a comparative analysis of justice in the case of black and white. This is a limited subject, because it omits from its focus a number of other dyads of injustice, including: women compared to men; undocumented immigrants compared to documented residents; disabled compared to abled; homeless compared to housed; extremely poor compared to affluent; nonblacks and nonwhites compared to whites and blacks. However, thinking about justice and injustice in the comparison of blacks to whites is an important stand-alone subject for at least two reasons. Comparative injustice to American blacks has a very long history that includes the broadly recognized injustice of slavery and the oblivion of many American whites to the conditions under which American blacks now live. The comparative disadvantage of American blacks continues to cough up shocking and horrible events, such as the police homicides of Oscar Juliuss Grant III, Trayvon Martin, Eric Garner, Michael Brown, Tamir Rice, and many others, unarmed, unaware, unprotected, gunned down on the streets and byways of twenty-first-century America, with the full force of the law, before and after.

How many others? Jaeah Lee, writing for *Mother Jones* in August 2014, notes that federal databases are incomplete, because they track only police use of force and deaths related to arrests. Also, data from police departments is scattered and incomplete, and there is no agency charged with precise recording of police shootings or killings of unarmed people. In 2007, *Colorlines* and the *Chicago Reporter* found that there was a "disproportionate number" of killings of blacks by police in New York, San Diego, and Las Vegas. The NAACP reported that out of forty-five police shootings in Oakland, California, over 2004-2008, thirty-seven of those shot were black, none were white, and fifteen died.[2] Kevin Johnson, Meghan Hoyer, and Brad Heath, writing for *USA TODAY*, reported that from 2005-2012, a white police officer killed a black person about twice a week; 18 percent of the blacks killed were under 21, compared to 8.7 percent of whites killed. Police reports of killings are voluntary and unaudited.[3] Most observers claim that the high profile cases of unarmed young black men killed by police are the tip of an iceberg. A 2013 report, "Operation Ghetto Storm," from the Malcolm X Grassroots Movement, states that 313 African Americans were killed by police in 2012, or "one every 28 hours," and that an incident of racial profiling preceded 43 percent of these killings.[4] A fact check of police records, prompted because only one nonacademic researcher had compiled the "Operation Ghetto Storm" report, led Katie Sanders for *Tampa Bay Times* to conclude that only 136 of the 313 were unarmed.[5] However, even the high profile cases alone are too many, so despite the importance of accurate records to track trends, they are not required in order to identify a serious problem.

The provision in assuming that U.S. blacks are treated unjustly compared to whites is that the relevant nature of justice and injustice must be explicated and clarified. That is a more complicated theoretical task than calling black chattel slavery, racially segregated education, or police racial profiling "unjust," would indicate. Many believe that these practices were and are unjust, but the question is, Why? Throughout the history of western political philosophy, there have in principle been two approaches to justice: Justice as an ideal and justice as the correction of injustice.

JUSTICE AS A PARTISAN IDEAL

The construction of justice as an ideal has dominated discussion from Plato to John Rawls, through Thomas Hobbes, John Locke, Jean-Jacques Rousseau, Georg Wilhelm Friedrich Hegel, Karl Marx, and John Stuart Mill—to name some canonical figures in Western political philosophy. In ways that cut through the social contract tradition that government should be based on the consent of those governed and for their benefit, the construction of justice as an ideal has benefited different groups in society. August and revered philosophers have represented the interests of now one and now another of these groups: an aristocratic intellectual elite (Plato), monarchists (Hobbes), a rising land-owning aristocracy (Locke), Swiss canton burghers (Rousseau), Prussian royalists (Hegel), workers (Marx), the British middle class electorate (Mill), and finally, to cap it all off in a stunning return to Plato, the intellectual elite (Rawls). In slight divergence but historical congruence with this tradition, St. Augustine and St. Aquinas represented the interests of the Catholic Church in political Christian theodicies deferring justice to heaven. And both early modern and modern emphases on the importance of laboring and production, have Protestant inflections in the writings of John Locke, Adam Smith, and perhaps despite himself, [the ideological atheist] Karl Marx. Altogether, these descriptions of ideal justice that favor only some groups have resulted in the neglect of real injustice by canonical philosophers.

I have told a lengthy story that is parallel to this précis of the history of western ideas about justice, about the absence of ideas of universal human equality in *The Ethics and Mores of Race: Equality After the History of Philosophy.*[6] However, neither a summary of that account, nor detailed explication of this claim about the beneficiaries represented in varied historical constructions of justice as an ideal, is necessary to proceed with the present analysis.

IDEAL JUSTICE AS A THEORY OF JUSTICE AND RAWLS

Even if it were not the case that justice as a partisan ideal has recrudesced over the history of philosophy, it remains true that no society has existed throughout the real history accompanying the tradition, which fully instantiates or realizes an ideal of justice for all members of that society. It needs to be clearly understood that justice as an ideal described or constructed by political philosophers is always *a theory of justice.* And, of course, no one makes this more clear than John Rawls, in chapter 1 of *A Theory of Justice.* After his initial description of the "veil of ignorance," behind which the basic institutions and principles of a society are chosen by stakeholders without knowledge of what their interests are in that society, that is, whether they are rich, poor, of high IQ, and so forth, Rawls specifies how we are to justify a "particular description of the original position." We are required to:

> See if the principles which would be chosen match our considered convictions of justice or extend them in an acceptable way. We can note whether applying these principles would

lead us to make the same judgments about the basic structure of society which we now make intuitively and in which we have the greatest confidence; or whether, in cases where our present judgments are in doubt and given with hesitation, these principles offer a resolution which we can affirm on reflection. . . . We check an interpretation of the initial situation, then, by the capacity of its principles to accommodate our firmest convictions and to provide guidance where guidance is needed.[7]

Rawls explains that if there is a discrepancy between our "considered convictions" and principles generated by our description of the initial situation, we have a choice:

We can either modify the account of the initial situation or we can revise our existing judgments, for even the judgments we take provisionally as fixed points are liable to revision. . . . Eventually we shall find a description of the initial situation that both expresses reasonable conditions and yields principles which match our considered judgments duly pruned and adjusted."[8]

The process described by Rawls is classic theory building. The principles yielded by our description of the initial situation are analogous to a scientific theory in explaining our considered convictions, which are, in turn, analogous to observational data. (We create a theory of justice to account for our existing beliefs about justice.) When new candidates for convictions are derived from the theory, these new convictions are analogous to predictions, which are either confirmed by our acceptance of them, or if rejected, lead to a redescription of the initial situation, that is, the theory. (If the theory says we should believe X, when we do not believe X, we can either bring ourselves to believe X or else change the theory.) There are many problems with Rawlsian ideal theory, but that is not the issue, here. I merely wish to emphasize its nature as a *theory*.[9]

Any theoretical ideal of justice, or any theory of justice, is compatible with just treatment of some in society that does not extend to all in society, because it is a normative theory and not a description of reality. Those who are treated justly in reality and whose interests are represented in the varied theories of ideal justice have, since the modern period, been mostly racially white; and those to whom justice has not been extended in reality have been disproportionately nonwhite. As a result, all of these theories of justice, which have been constructed by white males, are ultimate instances of white privilege—they have been created by whites and they privilege whites in reality, if not in explicit intent. As is true of all instances of white privilege, such ideal theories of justice are both logically and practically compatible with the unjust treatment of nonwhites. It follows from this structure that, as Charles Mills has pointed out, many mainstream contemporary white philosophers continue to be engaged in explicating, extending, and perfecting such idols, in the versions of "Rawlsland" [Mills's term] that they are privileged to inherit as part of the philosophical work in the profession that compels their attention (because it is so intellectually fascinating, and for the sake of their career advancement and career consolidation). Mills castigates these Elves of Rawls [my term] for their oblivion to racial injustice in U.S. society.[10] But that may not be altogether fair, because the work on theories of ideal justice is by its very nature separate from the other tradition of justice to which racial injustice belongs, namely correction of injustice. Mills thinks it was Rawls's intention to address injustice, for which his theory of justice was the "antechamber to the real hall of debate."[11] But, when an antechamber is 607 pages long, I think it qualifies to be regarded as the real hall.

JUSTICE AS THE CORRECTION OF INJUSTICE

Ideas of justice as the correction of injustice do not rise to high theory. They are not the subject of serious, white, manly, Ivy League PhD dissertations in Philosophy or the fruits of high quality minds, according to those who monitor the main halls of academic philosophy. A study of justice as the correction of injustice proceeds from the simple aspirations noted in the preface: those who are innocent will be left alone by the government, as represented by the police, and those who are guilty, such as the police in killing wrongfully, will be punished. Actually, in the present case, they are aspirations for black Americans, only. For white Americans they are expectations—predictions, even. The initial focus in studying justice as the correction of injustice is on particular, concrete social ills and oppressions and not on the kinds of pre-existing convictions about what is just, which Rawls called for in the deliberations necessary to activate his thought experiment. With the exception of John Stuart Mill's *On the Subjection of Women* and *The Communist Manifesto* by Marx and Engels, it is difficult to find revered texts in standard western history of political philosophy that begin with conditions of injustice. Rousseau flirts with that beginning ("Man is born free but he is everywhere in chains") but his real interest culminates in a utopian republic (i.e., *The Social Contract*), complete with a common will, where some must be compelled to be free.

The use of utopian visions to push for selected social interests is changing in light of more deflationary analyses of government from writers such as Giorge Agamben and Amartya Sen (although Sen, a student of Rawls, is an economist and not a political philosopher), as well as many who write about racial injustice, injustice to women, poverty, disability, exploitation, militarization, and so forth.[12] And there are strong voices in U.S. philosophy, for instance, Sally Haslanger's methodological project of approaching social injustice through the idea of unintended but determining "social meanings."[13] However it may be done and whatever its subject, beginning with concrete injustice and ending with proposals for its correction is a very open-ended and indeterminate task. But it might be the main subject of justice about which people who focus on real life and history genuinely care. There are also important intellectual antecedents in American history. Philosophical thought has a real history, in real life, as an essential survival tool for black Americans. Lucius Outlaw writes in the entry for "Africana Philosophy," in the *Stanford Encyclopedia of Philosophy*:

> The survival and endurance of conditions of racialized and gendered colonization, enslavement, and oppression—not conditions of leisured freedom—*compelled* more than a few African and African-descended persons to philosophize. Almost daily, even on what seemed the most mundane of occasions, oppressed Black people were *compelled* to consider the most fundamental existential questions: . . . Die at one's own initiation? Or, capitulate to dehumanization? Or, struggle to find and sustain faith and hope for a better life, on earth as well as in the afterlife, through creativity and beauty in speech, dance, and song while at work and rest; in thought and artistry; in finding and making truth and right; in seeking and doing justice; in forging and sustaining relations of family and community when such relations were largely prohibited; in rendering life sacred?[14]

In a more formal, international context, the Preamble to the United Nations' 1948 Universal Declaration of Human Rights (UDHR), which was written by a group of scholars that included philosophers[15] expresses a concern about injustice:

> Whereas disregard and contempt for human rights have resulted in barbarous acts which have outraged the conscience of mankind, and the advent of a world in which human beings shall enjoy freedom of speech and belief and freedom from fear and want has been proclaimed as the highest aspiration of the common people,
>
> Whereas it is essential, if man is not to be compelled to have recourse, as a last resort, to rebellion against tyranny and oppression, that human rights should be protected by the rule of law.[16]

Nowhere in UDHR do its authors define human rights, say where they come from, or put forth a positive, comprehensive theory of justice. The urgency of the universal human rights proclaimed is vaguely referred to individual human dignity based on common membership in a human family: "Whereas recognition of the inherent dignity and of the equal and inalienable rights of all members of the human family is the foundation of freedom, justice and peace in the world."[17] Readers of UDHR are not told that human rights are absolute and that it is morally right to recognize them and politically right to protect them. Rather, the readers of UDHR are warned that, because human rights are the "highest aspiration of the common people," disregard and contempt for them in an absence of protection by law, will result in "rebellion against tyranny and oppression." In other words, human rights must be respected as a condition for peace. The argument in UDHR is thus pragmatic and its subject is human rights as something that must be protected in order to have peace. The subtext is that human rights have been violated in the past and should not continue to be violated. Although the language of justice and injustice does not lead the discussion in this general preamble to specific rights, the focus of the entire document is on human rights that were unjustly violated during and just after World War II, and continue to be violated, today. Recognizing UDHR's origins in apprehensions of injustice is not the same thing as pretending that the declaration has been an *effective* statement of an ideal, or that it does much more than continue to inspire, but simply to note that the purpose of the document is to address and prevent injustice.

THE THEORY OF APPLICATIVE JUSTICE

Work on race and justice considered together, within political philosophy in the United States, has, again as Mills points out, appeared in the margins of the tradition of constructions of ideal justice.[18] The reason is that since the mid-twentieth century, this work has consisted of analysis and solutions to problems of continuing injustice. Many writers do not always pause to state their pre-existing background convictions or assumptions about the nature of justice that are at stake. Others self-consciously work in what is called "Rawlsian nonideal theory."[19] Overall there is a strong tendency in the discourse of black-white race relations, as a subject in academic philosophy, to start with attention to some real-life injustice, such as overt racism, institutional racism, identities forged in resistance to racism, racist stereotypes of nonwhites, and racial myths and scripts involving nonwhites. (The present attention to specific contemporary instances of racial profiling and police homicide is an even more specific instance of this trend.)

All of the philosophical analyses of race and justice considered together, proceed from comparative starting points: American blacks are disproportionately worse off *compared to* whites in important measures of human well-being and success in society as we know it; American blacks are held in low regard and treated disrespectfully *compared to* how American whites are regarded and treated. Assuming equally distributed human abilities, aptitudes, and talents, this situation is perceived as unfair regarding real unequal opportunities for social and economic entitlements, and unjust when political rights are violated. However, such discourse has so far been a long antechamber that fails to identify itself as the main hall. When justice is addressed in comparative ways, beginning with the unjust situations of some compared to the just situations of others, the subject is *applicative justice*. The conception of applicative justice relevant here refers to a cluster of societal and legal facts and normative requirements: Whites are treated justly by government, for the most part. Blacks are treated unjustly by government in enough instances to constitute injustice. Blacks should be treated by government as whites are treated. Notice that no ideal theory of justice is required here, but simply measures to bring the treatment of blacks in law, and by law enforcement officials, on a par with the treatment of whites.[20]

Notice, also, that there is an asymmetry between what counts for just and unjust treatment for groups. For a group to be treated justly, most members, or a high proportion of a group, need to be treated justly. But for a group to be treated unjustly, it is sufficient if a smaller number or lower proportion than required to meet the standard of just treatment, be treated unjustly. I believe that the reason for this asymmetry is that just treatment is easily normalized within communities, whereas unjust treatment of only a few is disruptive and considered abnormal among other members of their group. There is not only the disruption to daily life caused by the unjust treatment of a small number, a disruption that ripples out from their friends and relations. More problematically, if the group treated justly and the group treated unjustly belong to the same larger collective, such as whites and blacks in the United States, then the unjust treatment of even a very small number of that total collective of residents or citizens disrupts the entire collective. That is especially true if the total collective has a shared ideology, or is supposed to have a shared ideology of something like "justice for all." Just a few cases of injustice that are strongly related to group membership are sufficient to destabilize the descriptive aspects of the entire collective (national) ideology. And it is that kind of disruption that calls forth both a theory of applicative justice, and its real life application.

PRESENT APPLICATIONS OF APPLICATIVE JUSTICE

Immediate bodily and emotional reactions that it is *wrong* for police to stop young black men and subject them to humiliating searches without probable cause are based on the fact that young white men are not treated that way. When white police officers are not punished for killing unarmed young black men, after they have racially profiled them in such ways, it is perceived to be *unjust* according to standards for retributive justice that are routinely upheld when unarmed whites are killed. American whites who are innocent of crimes have little to fear from their local police in such regard. There are no high profile cases of unarmed white teenagers being gunned down for no reason, days before they are scheduled to attend college. Should that happen, it would be a terrible mistake, a punishable offense, a disruption that would cause immediate changes in whatever the police policies were, as well as profound apologies to surviving family members, from all officials concerned. Along these lines, Michelle Alexander in *The New Jim Crow*, writes:

> Can we envision a system that would enforce drug laws almost exclusively among young White men and largely ignore drug crime among Black men? Can we imagine young White men being rounded up for minor drug offenses, placed under the control of the criminal justice system, and then subjected to a lifetime of discrimination, scorn, and exclusion? Can we imagine this happening while [imagining] most Black men landed decent jobs or trotted off to college?[21]

Janine Jones poses the same question in terms of George Zimmerman's acquittal for killing Trayvon Martin:

> In U.S. society, as it is actually configured, can we imagine an armed Black man pursuing a young White boy, killing him because, allegedly, he felt threatened by the White boy, who was running away from him, and subsequently, on his testimony alone, being given a pass by the State's Attorney's Office to walk free, allegedly because there was not enough evidence to make an arrest? . . . Vanessa Wills recounts how she asked her students just such a question. Her classroom rippled with laughter. Wills interpreted that laughter to convey the students' recognition of the impossibility of the scenario.[22]

Wills writes that it was "nervous laughter" that followed this account:

> A big, black man, in a van, with a loaded gun, spots a white teenage boy walking in his neighbourhood wearing a hoodie. The black man reports the "suspicious" teenager to the police and then follows him, carrying his gun. The white teenager is shot and killed, and the black man reports that he feared for his life and was forced to shoot the teen in order to protect him-

self. The police conduct a cursory investigation and release the
man back onto the street within hours, no charges filed.[23]

Wills is here writing about presumed black guilt and she interprets
the student laughter to be a reaction to the idea that a "big black
man" would not *automatically* be an object of fear and suspicion.
If the students who laughed were white, they may have been nervous because of the comparison in treatment of blacks and whites.
Wills's posit of "presumed black guilt" is an expansion of how
police racial profiling works, to a general idea in the minds of most
white Americans, presumably a vastly larger number than those
who are police officers. But let's take a look at the numbers. In
2008, the 1.1 million police personnel in the United States were
251 per 100,000 of the population.[24] In 2008, there were about
250 million whites out of a total population of about 300 million.[25]
Wills's posit would entail that 251 out of about 250,000 could
influence the rest, an instance of about 1 person influencing 1,000.
That is not inconceivable, considering that police officers are active and fully functioning adults and that their leaders are also
often community leaders, or at least influential voices in their
communities, whereas the total white population would include
children, elderly, variably ill, and disabled. Consider further that
in 2008, a presidential election year, only 98.6 million whites
voted, which can be taken as a measure of civic engagement. That
is, the number of engaged whites was less than 100 million. So,
returning to the earlier police personnel figure of 1.1 million, each
police official would need to have influence on only about 100
other whites, roughly speaking, if we can assume that nonwhite
police officers and whites who do not support racial profiling
would balance each other out.[26] Thus, Wills's posit could be a
confirmable empirical hypothesis.

Applicative justice would seek to bring the legal treatment of
American blacks on a par with the legal treatment of American
whites. The rest of this chapter will proceed with descriptions of
some specific instances of these present injustices, with discussion
of broader cultural factors, followed by analyses of the U.S. Su-

preme Court reasoning that legitimizes police homicide following initial racially-profiled stops and frisks.

TRAYVON MARTIN AND GEORGE ZIMMERMAN

The case of Trayvon Martin was the first in a series of high profile tragedies that have burst the "blue bubble" of the lesser day of life in U.S. race relations, to unveil how blacks are treated unjustly in practices that remain legal. The 2012 fatal shooting of Trayvon Martin, an unarmed seventeen-year-old, by George Zimmerman, a neighborhood watch captain in Sanford, Florida, did not initially result in criminal charges against Zimmerman, because of Florida's "stand your ground" law.[27] Zimmerman had thought that Martin looked suspicious and he followed him. A violent confrontation between the two ensued, which ended when Zimmerman shot and killed Martin.

When Zimmerman was tried for second degree murder, in 2013, an all-female jury acquitted him of both that charge and the lesser charge of manslaughter. There was widescale public outcry that Zimmerman had racially profiled and stalked Martin, who had committed no crime, with no evidence that he intended to commit any crime. Martin was on his way home to his father's house, in a light rain. He had bought a can of soda and a bag of Skittles for his brother, both of which were in his pocket, and he was talking on his cell phone to a female friend. The rain had prompted him to pull up the hood of his black jersey, making him an iconographic, but it turned out, also stereotypical young, black, male in motion.[28]

The procedures of existing retributive justice were followed. It was widely reported that Florida's "stand your ground" law permitted the police who responded to the homicide to initially accept Zimmerman's claim of self-defense. This led to protests by representatives of the Martin family and others. Charges of criminal homicide and second degree murder were brought against Zimmerman, several months later. At the trial, over a year later, the jury was given the following definitions of the charges in its instructions: For second degree murder, the jury had to find, beyond a reasonable doubt, that "there was an unlawful killing of Trayvon Martin by an act imminently dangerous to another and demonstrating a depraved mind without regard for human life." For manslaughter, the jury had to find, beyond a reasonable doubt, that "George Zimmerman intentionally committed an act or acts that caused the death of Trayvon Martin."[29] It was not unlawful for Zimmerman to follow Martin, because he was a neighborhood watch captain (although the 911 operator had instructed him not to leave his vehicle.[30]) The circumstances supporting his claim of self-defense, which included his internal skull fracture when the police arrived, were allowed to be taken into account. If the jury found that Zimmerman's killing of Martin was an act of self-defense, then he would have acted lawfully and could not be found guilty of either second degree murder or manslaughter. Zimmerman was found not guilty of both charges.

THE INJUSTICE OF ZIMMERMAN'S ACQUITTAL

Public expressions of outrage that followed the delay in Zimmerman's arrest and then his acquittal, were centered on the injustice of Zimmerman's racial profiling of Martin. Because Martin was black, Zimmerman regarded him as suspicious and followed him with a handgun that he was evidently prepared to use, not because he did use it, but because he was an auxiliary policeman, already armed with a gun and a strong belief that he was a hero.[31] Many believed that Zimmerman did not regard or treat Martin the same as he would have had Martin not been black, which led to his unjust killing of Martin, so that his acquittal was unjust. These judgments and the attendant indignation at injustice implicitly appealed, not to positive law or to the existing theory of retributive justice that was legally applied, but to a principle of human equality: *All human beings are morally equal and have equal intrinsic value*. It is largely assumed that principle is backed up by the U.S.

legal principle of *equal treatment under the law*, specifically, the Equal Protection Clause of the Fourteenth Amendment. The assumption that there is or should be equal treatment under the law is made by most Americans, including those who have never heard of the Fourteenth Amendment, because the United States is supposed to be a color blind society with "equality under the law." If Martin was treated differently, because he was black, both the general equality principle and the Equal Protection Clause were violated. Many thought that Zimmerman was wrong to kill Martin and that Zimmerman's failure to be convicted was wrong. They were shocked to learn that the legal system did not respond as they did.

Petitions were signed.[32] Rallies across the United States, one week after the jury's verdict, attested to the strength of the public's indignation at the perceived injustice. Demonstrators at these rallies explicitly called for justice.[33] The NAACP asked the U.S. Attorney General to prosecute Zimmerman for a hate crime.[34] (That request may have been disingenuous, because as discussed in chapter 2, it should have been obvious to any lawyer at the time that Zimmerman shooting Martin did not meet the standards of a hate crime.) Well over a year later, there has been no federal action, either against Zimmerman's acquittal, or the acquittal of a number of additional high profile police homicides following racial profiling.

Some people thought that Zimmerman's following of Martin, after the 911 operator had told him to remain in his vehicle, was a form of stalking. However, according to Florida law, the crime of stalking requires malicious intent and repeated following or harassing, whereas Zimmerman only followed Martin once, because he suspected him of being a criminal.[35] So, according to Florida law, Zimmerman did not stalk Martin.

If we assume that the prosecutor did not produce sufficient evidence that Zimmerman acted with "depraved mind disregard for human life" and also failed to prove that Zimmerman formed an intent to kill Martin, then, if we accept the state's definition of these crimes—and there is no choice here because that is a matter of hard, existing law—there is no legal problem with the jury's verdict, as the laws now stand. The perception of injustice in the jury's verdict is based on a combination of prior injustices: Zimmerman had racially profiled Martin, assuming his criminality, beforehand; Zimmerman was armed and Martin was unarmed; Zimmerman was acting like a police officer, although he was merely a neighborhood watch captain. While it is odd that the jury was not concerned about Zimmerman's authority, the real problem lies with the nature of police authority he was emulating.

We have to try to understand why Zimmerman's jury did not find Zimmerman guilty. The jury, like other juries and grand juries, accepted as just what some onlookers considered unjust: prior racial suspicion and profiling, a right to follow a suspect, and a naturalness in killing a suspect under those circumstances. It is as though the jury accepted a "frame" that identified Zimmerman as a righteous hunter! If Zimmerman had a right to be that hunter in the view of the jury, then he would have a right to kill Martin, because skilled and righteous hunters kill their prey.

THE HUNTING SCHEMA

A schema is a psychological combination of pre-existing beliefs, contextual events or conditions, and actions, such that the existence of the beliefs in a relevant context *predisposes* an individual to act in certain ways. On a visceral, or bodily and emotional level, which accompanies the pseudo-rational suspicion of criminality (discussed in chapter 2, as tied to race-based rates of incarceration), young African-American males are uniquely picked out as dangerous prey that young white males are permitted to hunt in some circumstances. The hunting schema kicks in when racial profiling is kicked up from routine intrusive surveillance to a violent or potentially violent encounter.

Racial profiling itself already has emotional and physical components that can over-ride even the most racially-neutral police training. Broad cultural stereotypes about dangerous young black males evoke fear, generally, and there is no reason to believe that white police officers and auxiliary police personnel are immune to such fear—their fear mirrors, as well as it influences, fear in the wider white population. Evidence for the pervasiveness of such antiblack criminal stereotypes has been documented by the experiences of black males such as Barack Obama and George Yancy (related in chapters 1 and 2). Another part of the emotional aspect of racial profiling concerns the self-image or personal identity of the police themselves. In the context of discussions of police discretion, some writers advocate an objective approach, whereby police would be trained to distinguish between their subjective responses to situations and their professional roles as police officers.[36]

However, in American culture, there is a kind of heroic personal identity associated with the role of police officers. Courage and protectiveness are high virtues for the American police, visible in actions that receive civic honor, as well as in characters and deeds featured in popular entertainment. Moreover, such courage and protectiveness is closely bound up with male gender identity, especially for young men who work with their bodies. Consider the ages of officers who have recently killed young black men in high profile cases: Oscar Julius Grant III, twenty-two, and Johannes Mehserle, twenty-seven; Trayvon Martin, seventeen, and George Zimmerman, twenty-nine; Eric Garner, forty-four, and Daniel Pantaleo, twenty-nine; Michael Brown, eighteen, and Darren Wilson, twenty-eight; Tamir Rice, twelve, and Timothy Loehmann, twenty-six. Except for Eric Garner, all of these victims were under thirty and they were significantly younger than their killers. Youth itself, whether recognized or not—Zimmerman thought Martin was older than seventeen and Loehmann's partner reported Rice as "about twenty"—is a form of comparative vulnerability. Garner, a father of four, who left a widow and mother, was disabled by obesity and asthma. More striking, the police officers were all under thirty.

Stop and frisks are also hands-on. Shoving people against walls, knocking them to the ground, searching their persons, and asking them to take their clothes off, are all aggressively intimate. Behavior of this kind, including hunting, are young men's activities. One group of elders crafts the rules and sends the young officers out; another group of elders, or at least mature people on juries, understandingly forgives the occasionally disastrous consequences. The young black men who are killed are unwitting victims, of an unrestrained, predatory, cultural practice of young men in the United States. Such episodes of legal homicide reflect or are reflected in a genre of human entertainment that has existed at least since 1924—humans hunting humans.[37] (Some students of the history of race relations in the United States may not consider it coincidental that this genre began as lynching was phasing out.[38]) The hunting of humans by other humans would be criminal homicide in most other contexts. But in the context of young white police officers killing young black males, it is protected by prosecutors, judges, and juries, and accepted by the majority of the white majority, because of respect for the authority of the police and widespread belief, based on the disproportional imprisonment of blacks, that young black males are likely to be criminals, indeed *dangerous animals* according to long-standing racist mythology.

In contemporary encounters between police officers and young black men, *the hunting schema* is a staple of American culture that is activated in a three-part sequence of actions and events. First, procedurally-sanctioned criminal suspicion of a young black man is followed by a police officer in stopping or attempting to stop the suspect. Second, stopping or attempting to stop the suspect results in a physical confrontation between officer and suspect, an attempt of the suspect to flee, with the officer in pursuit, or a surrender of the suspect, who either lies on the ground or remains upright with his hands up. Or, the suspect may be shot without even fully realizing he was under suspicion, as was Tamir Rice. Killing a passive victim is usually unconscionable in civilized society, but in hunting scenarios, the prey has already been identified as prey, before the act of killing. Third, the officer shoots to kill and kills the young black suspect. It doesn't matter if the suspect is running toward or away from the officer, is actively resisting, or passively submitting. The hunter kills his prey, because he is the hunter, the prey is the prey, and that is what must happen. This sequence plays out in all the recent high profile cases. Tamir Rice's fate was discussed in chapter 1 and the details of what happened to Trayvon Martin are already known. So we turn now to Oscar Grant III, Michael Brown, and Eric Garner.

OSCAR JULIUSS GRANT III

In July, 2013, soon after Zimmerman's acquittal, the documentary "Fruitvale Station," was released, which depicts the life of Oscar Juliuss Grant III, a twenty-two-year-old black man, who was shot by Johannes Mehserle, a transit police officer, at the Fruitvale BART (Bay Area Rapid Transit) station in Oakland California on January 1, 2009.[39] Grant had been arrested four times since he was eighteen and spent the last two years in prison. January 1 was Grant's mother's birthday and the film depicts his last day. He bought crabs for his mother's gumbo dinner and talked about his plans to attend barber school, using a skill he had learned in prison.

A fight between Grant and an acquaintance started on a train headed toward Fruitvale Station. Accounts of what happened are conflicting and there were multiple video recordings. Officers Tony Pirone and Marysol Domenici rounded up Grant and four of his friends. When Pirone and Mehserle forced Grant to the ground, a friend of Grant's, who had been videorecording at a distance of about ten feet, later said that Grant was cooperating and begging them not to shoot. Mehserle shot Grant once in the back, while he was on the ground. Mehserle later testified tearfully that he thought he was reaching for his Taser weapon, instead of his gun. Although many people who had arrived at the Fruitvale Station on the same train witnessed the shooting, police officers who subsequently responded did not question observers before they dispersed, because it was not immediately known to their supervisors that a fatal shooting had occurred.

Mehserle was charged with second degree murder and voluntary manslaughter, but convicted of involuntary manslaughter; Pirone was fired and later charged with unemployment fraud.[40,41] Mehserle received a two year sentence but was released for good behavior after eleven months. He and four others were cleared on charges of using "excessive brutality," in the incident leading up to Grant's death.[42]

THE DEATH OF MICHAEL BROWN

According to CNN and other news reports, Michael Brown, eighteen, and Dorian Johnson, twenty-two, were walking in the middle of the street, heading to Johnson's house, when Officer Wilson stopped them, saying, "Get the fuck on the sidewalk" or "Get the fuck out of the street." Brown and Johnson said they were close to their destination and would be out of the street very soon. Wilson drove away, stopped, and rushed toward them in reverse. There was a tussle as Wilson's car door was opened, either by Wilson or Brown. Brown's upper body was in the patrol car, either because he was attacking Wilson or Wilson had pulled him in. Wilson shot Brown in the hand. Brown ran and Wilson pursued him. Johnson hid behind a car.

Johnson told *CNN*'s Wolf Blitzer: "I saw the officer proceeding after my friend Big Mike with his gun drawn, and he fired a second shot and that struck my friend Big Mike. . . . And at that time, he turned around with his hands up, beginning to tell the officer that he was unarmed and to tell him to stop shooting. But at that time, the officer fired several more shots into my friend, and he hit the ground and died."

Josie, described as "a purported friend of the family" who was relaying what Wilson's "significant other" said, provided this account: "Michael takes off with his friend. They get to be about thirty-five feet away and Darren [Wilson], of course protocol is to pursue. So he stands up and yells, "Freeze!" Michael and his friend turn around and Michael starts taunting him. "Oh, what are you going to do about it? You're not gonna shoot me." . . . And then he said all of a sudden [Brown] just started to bum rush him. He just started coming at him full speed so [Wilson] he just started shooting and he just kept coming. So he [Wilson] really thinks he [Brown] was on something because he just kept coming. It was unbelievable. And then so he finally ended up, the final shot was in the forehead and then he fell about two, three feet in front of the officer."[43]

The St. Louis County Grand Jury deliberated over whether to indict Wilson, from August 20 to November 25, 2014. They convened for seventy hours of testimony, from sixty witnesses, including that of Wilson. Wilson at 6'4" and 210 lbs, to Brown's 6'4" 290 lbs, said that in the car tussle, he feared for his life and felt like "a five-year-old holding onto Hulk Hogan." There was conflicting testimony on whether Brown was charging Wilson when he was shot, or trying to surrender. Wilson shot at Brown a total of ten times, perhaps six in their final encounter, the fatal shot to the top of his head.[44]

The grand jury concluded that they did not have sufficient evidence to indict Wilson of any charges (nine of their twelve would have had to agree to indict), although Prosecutor Robert McCulloch did not present them with any specific charges to consider, which is unusual in prosecutor–grand jury relations. Additional aspects of the procedure have been considered unusual by legal observers: Most of the jury's documents, including testimony, were made public,[45] giving the procedure an aspect of a trial, rather than a decision to indict. Quoted by those who thought the trial aspect of the procedure irregular was U.S. Supreme Court Justice Antonin Scalia, who had explained the traditional role of a grand jury in the Opinion he wrote for *United States v. Williams*, in 1992[46]:

> It is the grand jury's function not "to enquire . . . upon what foundation [the charge may be] denied," or otherwise to try the suspect's defenses, but only to examine "upon what foundation [the charge] is made" by the prosecutor. (*Respublica v. Shaffer*,

1 Dall. 236 (O. T. Phila. 1788); see also F. Wharton, *Criminal Pleading and Practice* § 360, pp. 248-249 (8th ed. 1880). As a consequence, neither in this country nor in England has the suspect under investigation by the grand jury ever been thought to have a right to testify or to have exculpatory evidence presented.[47]

"I CAN'T BREATHE"

Eric Garner's death after police officers tried to arrest him on Staten Island for selling "loosies" or single untaxed cigarettes, was declared a homicide by the medical examiner's office on August 1, 2014, with contributing factors of obesity, asthma, and high blood pressure. Garner had been arrested previously for the same offense and was recorded as saying on the day he died, "Every time you see me, you want to mess with me. I'm tired of it. It stops today. I'm minding my business. Please just leave me alone."[48]

A seven-minute video clip shows Pantaleo shoving Garner's face into the concrete, in what onlookers described as a chokehold, because it blocked his windpipe. Emergency Medical Technicians (EMTs) arrive four minutes into that clip, but do nothing to aid Garner. Garner says, "I can't breathe," at least ten times.[49] Officer Daniel Pantaleo, who had been accused of false arrest and violation of police procedures in two previous lawsuits, was relieved of his badge and gun and placed on desk duty; four EMTs were also suspended without pay.[50]

On November 21, 2014, Pantaleo told the grand jury that he had not been aware that Garner was in mortal danger and he called what others saw as a chokehold, a "takedown maneuver." The Staten Island Grand Jury had access to three different videotapes of Garner's death. The grand jury, composed of half whites and the other half black and Hispanic, released its decision—unanimity was required—not to indict Pantaleo on December 3, 2014.[51] Observers have stated that this grand jury was especially unlikely to indict, because Staten Island residents, who are

70 percent non-Hispanic white, are more supportive of NYPD officers than those in any other borough of New York City and generally believe that the NYPD treats people of different races equally.[52]

THE LEGALITY OF STOP AND FRISK AND POLICE FORCE

Protests and demonstrations, "die-ins," and national and local conversations continued through most of December 2014. The grand jury decisions in Brown and Garner, the trial decisions for Martin and Grant, and, as will likely be the case for legal proceedings regarding Rice, are not perceived as just. Federal, state, and congressional plans for further investigation have followed this public outcry, including plans for the use of body cameras by police. Whether there will be changes in how police homicide is dealt with juridically remains to be seen. While constitutional and statute law is explicit about equal rights, police discretion and immunity are protected by judges.

Two of the recent high profile cases considered here—Garner and Grant—are instances of stop and frisk procedures gone bad. Each year, U.S. police departments voluntarily report about 400 "justifiable police homicides" to the FBI, which is considered an incomplete record. Out of 2,600 justifiable homicides reported from 2005 to 2011, forty-one officers were charged with murder or manslaughter.[53] The reason the number of indictments are low, and may continue to be low, may rest on the U.S. Supreme Court 1989 Opinion in *Graham v. Connor*.[54]

Graham, a diabetic, asked his friend Berry to drive him to a convenience store to purchase orange juice. Graham saw that the store was crowded and hurried out again. Officer O'Connor thought that Graham's movements were suspicious and asked him and Berry to wait while he checked the store. Back-up officers arrived and handcuffed Graham, causing injuries. Graham sued, claiming that excessive force had been used in violation of his Fourteenth Amendment rights.

The Court held that all claims that enforcement officials have used excessive force must be analyzed under the Fourth Amendment's "objective reasonableness" standard, rather than a substantive due process standard requiring that "all government intrusions into fundamental rights and liberties be fair and reasonable and in furtherance of a legitimate government interest." The objective reasonableness standard is:

> whether the officers' actions are "objectively reasonable" in light of the facts and circumstances confronting them, without regard to their underlying intent or motivation. The "reasonableness" of a particular use of force must be judged from the perspective of a reasonable officer on the scene, and its calculus must embody an allowance for the fact that police officers are often forced to make split-second decisions about the amount of force necessary in a particular situation.[55]

U.S. police academies systematically teach "Graham Factors" for determining when lethal force may legitimately be used: How severe is the crime? Does the suspect pose an immediate threat to the safety of officers and others? Is the suspect resisting arrest or trying to flee?[56] Although the Garner grand jury decision not to indict would be difficult to justify according to *Graham*, because Garner was already on the ground, smothering, before he was choked, George Zimmerman and Darren Wilson's claims that they feared for their lives are legally supported by Graham, which held that police officers have the authority to decide when their lives are in danger and to determine "the amount of force necessary in a particular situation."

In *Plumhoff et al. v. Richard*, the U.S. Supreme Court ruled in 2013 that individuals' Fourth Amendment rights violations must be balanced against an official's *qualified immunity*, unless it can be shown that the official violated a statutory or constitutional right that was "clearly established" at the time of the challenged conduct.[57] Both *Graham* and *Plumhoff* constitute a change from a focus on the constitutional rights of citizens against unreasonable (that is unprovoked and unwarranted) search and seizure, to what it seems "reasonable" for police to do in the heat of a moment. Many Americans still believe that police officers are constrained to behave in ways that make the use of deadly force "a last resort." They may believe that the legal world is still governed by the 1984 U.S. Supreme Court ruling in *Tennessee v. Garner*, where the Court wrote, "The use of deadly force to prevent the escape of all felony suspects, whatever the circumstances, is constitutionally unreasonable."[58] By contrast, at this time, if "suspicious" people try to flee, it can be construed as "reasonable" that police kill them, because once labeled "suspicious," police can reason that the suspect poses a danger to other members of the community. Moreover, if police officers fear for their lives, then it becomes legally reasonable that they resort to deadly force, because their "underlying intent and motivation" are irrelevant to that standard.

The context of stop and frisk, itself, is the factor enabling the recent uses of deadly force that so many consider unjust. To understand the legality of that context, we need to go back to Chief Justice Earl Warren's 1968 Opinion in *Terry v. Ohio*.[59] Warren first distinguished between "stops" and "arrests," and "frisks" and "searches": "stops" are brief police interrogations based on suspicion and "arrests" are taking suspects into custody based on criminal evidence; "frisks" are determinations of whether the suspect has a weapon, restricted to superficial searches or "pat downs" of the surface of the body, undertaken for the officer's immediate safety; and "searches" are more invasive investigations that can be performed only after arrests. Mindful of the exclusionary rule requiring that criminal evidence be obtained lawfully, before an arrest, the Court narrowed its attention to "whether it is always unreasonable for a policeman to seize a person and subject him to a limited search for weapons unless there is probable cause for an arrest."[60] Warren went on to find that the Fourth Amendment protection against unreasonable searches and seizures applied as much to stops and frisks, as to arrests and searches: "We therefore reject the notions that the Fourth Amendment does not come into play at all as a limitation upon police conduct if the officers stop short of something called a 'technical arrest' or a 'full-blown search.'"[61] Warren then answers the question of how a Fourth Amendment intrusion is to be justified, with a "reasonable person" standard:

> The scheme of the Fourth Amendment becomes meaningful only when it is assured that at some point the conduct of those charged with enforcing the laws can be subjected to the more detached, neutral scrutiny of a judge who must evaluate the reasonableness of a particular search or seizure in light of the particular circumstances. And in making that assessment it is imperative that the facts be judged against an objective standard: would the facts available to the officer at the moment of the seizure or the search "warrant a man of reasonable caution in the belief" that the action taken was appropriate?[62]

Warren recognizes that the government has a general interest in crime detection and concludes, based on that interest, that "a police officer may in appropriate circumstances and in an appropriate manner approach a person for purposes of investigating possibly criminal behavior even though there is no probable cause to make an arrest."[63] Furthermore, "It does not follow that because an officer may lawfully arrest a person only when he is apprised of facts sufficient to warrant a belief that the person has committed or is committing a crime, the officer is equally unjustified, absent that kind of evidence, in making any intrusions short of an arrest." [64]

However strong the ultimate legal support from the U.S. Supreme Court may be—and it is ultimate—the law remains on vacation concerning racial bias in stops of black suspects, as well as racial bias that may exaggerate the danger posed by black suspects in moments of physical confrontation. Moreover, in some of the cases considered here—Trayvon Martin, Michael Brown, and Tamir Rice—there were no actual stops or frisks, but a direct escalation of violence toward death. If, as Warren stated, the interests of the government in preventing and detecting crime may override Fourth Amendment rights in actions by police in stops and frisks, does the same apply to attempted stops and frisks?

The reasonable officer standard may result in justifiable homicide if a police officer fears for his life, even if the officer has used bad judgment in creating a situation in which he put his life in danger. For example, Officer Christopher Manney shot Dontre Hamilton, age thirty-one, fourteen times after getting into a violent struggle with him in a downtown Milwaukee park in April 2014. Earlier, employees at a nearby Starbucks had called in a complaint against Hamilton for sleeping on a park bench. Two other police officers responded before Manney arrived and decided that no further police action was necessary. Manney was fired for incompetence in creating the altercation, but it was announced in December 2014 that no charges would be filed against him, because his actions were appropriate after he had created that altercation.[65]

Returning to the Opinion in *Graham*, underlying intent and motivation are not irrelevant to how human beings behave when race is involved in the United States. If the hunting schema hypothesis proposed earlier is also a factor, then the absence of law in attention to the basic human rights of black Americans in particular—where the effects of the law violate their rights—permits and connives with barbarous actions. Under the law, or alongside it, in the category of what the U.S. Supreme Court considers irrelevant to the "reasonable officer" standard, antiblack racism, as visceral or bodily and emotional, continues to operate. Racism as embodied is not a system of beliefs but a way of doing things that bypasses conscious and law-abiding beliefs.

Furthermore, the antecedent motives of police are not irrelevant. Officers may be biased against blacks and predisposed to view them as criminals, as racial profiling policies dictate. But what counts as bias or racism has changed over the past few decades, because it has become part of official public morality not to be a racist or have racist beliefs or attitudes. The result is that police officers may not know whether or not they are racially biased. Polite and tame philosophers engaged in the discourse of white privilege are amazed and astounded to encounter their own racism (as we have seen in chapter 1). It is therefore not a stretch to imagine that those who are not particularly sensitive to racism, or do not consider antiblack racism an ongoing problem, do not recognize their own racism.

Racism today often coexists with avowals of color blindness. Recent research in cognitive science suggests that people who are explicitly not racist, may nonetheless exhibit brain activity or reaction responses that indicate that they believe racist stereotypes are true. It has been fairly well confirmed that recognition of faces of those whose race is different from their own, is lower among whites than nonwhites. Also, whites are more likely than nonwhites to produce "startle responses" to facial pictures of those of races different from their own.[66] Research of this nature stands in for what used to be called "unconscious racism" and it is more scientific than past studies of "the unconscious." But unfortunately, it is very remote from what lawmakers, judges, juries, and grand juries take into account in assessing current instances of white police officer homicide cases with unarmed blacked victims, as well as police behavior during stops and frisks or attempts to perform them.

CONCLUSION

If you want peace, work for justice.

—Pope Paul VI [1]

This book has been exploratory. The injustice of U.S. police racial profiling and homicide has been found to be bounded by law, individual misinformation, distorted cultural associations of crime and race, and legacies of earlier injustice. And that is only part of the present problem. As of this writing, New York City has emerged as a microcosm of the dysfunction and turmoil that can follow police misconduct and public reactions to what is perceived to be unjust. On December 20, 2014, a mentally ill man killed two NYPD officers after referring to the Michael Brown and Eric Garner cases on social media. Members of the NYPD turned their back on Mayor de Blasio, when he went to the hospital where the slain police officers had been taken. The families of Eric Garner and Michael Brown repudiated any association with, or support for, the killings of the two police officers and offered condolences to their families. Patrick Lynch, fifteen-year President of the Patrolmen's Benevolent Association (PBA), the largest NYPD union, blamed Mayor de Blasio for the New York killings, because he had publically reported warning his biracial son about encounters with police, following the grand jury's failure to indict the officer who killed Eric Garner. Lynch said that de Blasio, was "running a fucking revolution rather than a city." Others, including former New York State Governor George Pataki, also blamed the mayor and Reverend Al Sharpton for their support of demonstrations against the Garner grand jury decision. Former Mayor Rudy Giuliani at first said that Mayor de Blasio could not be held responsible for the actions of the deranged killer, but he later blamed both him and President Obama for supporting the demonstrators by delivering a message that the police are bad and racist. Giuliani also insisted, as he had before, that 93 percent of black homicide victims are killed by other blacks. Racist hate commentary was on full display on the *Wall Street Journal*'s website following the story about the police officer killings. Demonstrators the day after the New York City police shootings took a more conciliatory tone than earlier. They added "Blue Lives Matter" to "Black Lives Matter." Instead of chanting "I Can't Breathe," they sang the children's gospel song "This Little Light of Mine." Sharpton emphasized that he did not support people taking the law into their own hands, but was working to change the system by making it more fair. The day after that, de Blasio called for a suspension of protests and demonstrations until after the slain police officers were buried.[2]

Overall, the present situation in New York City and beyond does not support optimism about an end to police racial profiling and homicide following stops and frisks, or their attempts. There are unlikely to be fast dramatic solutions to the underlying legal and social problems that have erupted into the recent events that prompted this book. Nevertheless, hope is a healthy attitude and violent response is not an option. No reasonable or sane voices in this ongoing crisis want more violence and that does speak positively to future solutions.

Recent U.S. Supreme Court opinions do not explicitly take racial bias into account, as the mental and emotional content of what may motivate individual police action. The Court's objective standards for what "a reasonable police officer" decides to do in what is perceived to be a dangerous situation, would inevitably defer to broad beliefs and attitudes within existing police culture.

Policies of racial profiling that are based on racial proportions in the prison population, rather than crime rates in areas being patrolled, have not been thoroughly challenged in the courts. American police officers remain within their legal rights to both practice racial profiling and shoot to kill while attempting stops and frisks, in the absence of probable cause. Indictments and guilty verdicts for police homicide of unarmed suspects are constrained by very broad police discretion and criminal laws that were designed for civilians and are preempted by that discretion. Definitive legal solutions to these problems are in need of new, brilliant, and dedicated lawyering, which will take years to succeed, and more years to effectively apply.

Applicative justice requires that the legal treatment of American blacks be brought on a par with that of American whites, beyond written law, into real life practice. Simply reiterating how whites are "privileged" is not an effective response on the part of concerned academics, because it merely reinscribes their white privileges into new white identities. Perceptions of current injustice rest on basic human rights that people value intuitively and call for in anguished protests and demonstrations, but without understanding how the American legal system fails to protect the rights of black Americans. It may be possible to improve the situation by correcting specific comparative injustices, before the relevant interpretations of constitutional law change, or even if they never do change. Institutional and government practices go far beyond what is formally written, into real life. Such practices can mirror formal law, be less just than it describes, or more just.

Many responsible and compassionate leaders and officials feel that they should do something, offer some reassurance to the disillusioned, some balm to the bereaved. When part of the population perceives injustice in specific harm or death to some of its members, it is essential that responsible leadership in all areas of public life offer consolation. Present blame, violent reaction, and protests and demonstrations have bypassed or denied the need for what should be a period of official nationwide (if not formally "national") mourning. The killing of innocent young people—Tamir Rice was a twelve-year-old child!—by government officials is a national concern, even if it is not acknowledged. It is a national concern because whites and nonwhites together make up the nation in which such events now occur and they draw their individual and collective identities from being members of that nation. Such sudden and unjust loss of life should be publically shared, during time respectfully set aside for sadness. It calls not only for black armbands, but for public memorials, communal prayer or meditation, and designated *silence*. Reactions of this nature should be immediate, but it is just as important that permanent public memorials be planned in honor of those killed, so that people do not forget wrongful deaths.[3]

After sadness and silence, immediate practical remedies should be designed for institutional and social change out of concern for the well-being of over 90 percent of the black population who are not criminals. Racial profiling or fear and suspicion is not primarily a moral matter for whites in terms of their moral virtues or vices, but an offense to blacks, as individual human beings. As Judge Shira Scheindlin stated, "No one should live in fear of being stopped whenever he leaves his home to go about the activities of daily life." So long as police racial profiling continues, concerned educators and other leaders of societal institutions can continue to host conversations for those who are not directly affected by it, to consider what it is like to live in such fear, for one's children and grandchildren, as well as oneself.[4]

Americans are not about to abandon their ideals concerning the police. Police officers, like military personnel, remain enshrined as sources of protection, heroism, and the kind of discipline that administers public order. It is not accidental that Wikipedia prefaces its 2014 alphabetical list of over five hundred police shows with, "Dramas involving police procedural work, and private detectives, secret agents, and the justice system have been a mainstay of broadcast television since the early days of broadcasting."[5] As popular entertainment, police television shows, movies, and fiction are usually morality plays, narratives of good triumphing over bad. People watch them as food for moral aspirations and the expression of shared intuitions about justice and glory. No matter how long it will take to bring the treatment by police of innocent young blacks on a par with their treatment of innocent young whites, no matter how difficult and bitter that struggle may be, police officers, like military personnel, will remain enshrined as sources of protection, heroism, and the kind of discipline that administers public order. But that doesn't mean they should not be recognized to have the same frailties of others, in beliefs and motivations that derive from antiblack cultural norms and myths, or that there are not ways in which they can become better, in how they regard and treat people of color, in their roles as first responders.

Not only are police officers first responders to crime, but they represent the entire legal and criminal justice system to members of the public in public places. For society to be orderly, it is essential that members of the public, especially young people, and especially young people who are not white, have good reason to believe that police officers will deal with them fairly. To criticize police practices is not the same thing as saying that all American police officers are bad people. In a democratic society, it must be possible for everyone in a position of power to accept criticism and be open to the possibility of change. Local police departments often create the impression of not distinguishing between being blameworthy and accepting responsibility. Blame is accusatory and may be avoided as dishonorable, whereas the acceptance of responsibility allows for future growth and honor. By the same token, just as it is not necessary "to burn the whole house down in order to get rid of the mice," neither is it necessary to rebuild the entire house in order to refurbish a damaged part. What many critics may correctly perceive as society-wide and historically deep antiblack racism in the United States does not have to be thoroughly corrected before the immediate issue of police killings of unarmed young black men can be addressed. The immaturity of some armed young police officers and their lack of experience in interacting with members of the communities they serve can be addressed by police administrators and supervisors, who have as much at stake in the public's trust of them, as the public does. The American police, as a professional community, appear to know this. Not one of the officers responsible for the death of innocent victims in the high profile cases has been lauded or honored by his peers. Most have resigned or been dismissed and that is an indication of responsiveness within police ranks, even if it is not part of their culture to readily and publicly admit wrongdoing.

The way that the Broken Window Policy has been implemented in major U.S. cities has failed to serve many members of communities it was designed to support, as totalities. Former New York City mayor Giuliani has reportedly brought attention to the fact that 93 percent of black homicide victims are killed by other blacks. While that fact is irrelevant to the issue of recent killings of unarmed young black men by young white police officers performing or attempting to perform stop and frisks, it is a major social problem. To the extent that it is a responsibility of the police to address, and it is insofar as their charge is to detect and prevent serious crime, it should be remembered and emphasized that stop and frisk policies were originally designed to be part of a much wider program that included *community policing*. The core idea in community policing is that members of police departments interact with members of high crime communities, to build community and prevent crime.[6] The importance of that idea lies in its ability to diffuse perceptions on the part of the public within and from these communities that the police are pitted against them as an occupying force. By the same token, attitudes on the part of the police that the prevention and detection of crime always or usually requires direct combat with criminals and suspects, require reexamination.

As offensive as stop and frisk policies are to those caught in their nets, the numbers of deadly escalations of attempts to stop and frisk can be considered against bigger numbers. As noted earlier, from 2002-2012, over 4.4 million stops and frisks were performed in New York City. At a rate of about 50 percent black suspects, this would amount to 220,000 stops of black suspects a year. Compared to nationwide estimates of 136-200 killings of blacks by police on a yearly basis, the odds of death for a black person from a police stop and frisk based on the New York City statistics would be at most near 1 in 1,000 each year. The odds are likely better on a national level, because New York City has a disproportionately large black population. Still, the odds of a black person being killed by a police officer are significantly higher than the likelihood of being killed in a car crash, which is 1 in 6,500 a year.[7]

Communities of color react to killings of unarmed young black men, symbolically and iconographically, as they should, because even one unjust race-related event creates an atmosphere of race-related injustice. Each unpunished killing is treated as a symbol of overall social injustice to whole communities of people of color. Attempts to suppress nonviolent expressions of outrage are disturbing insofar as they fail to respect human sensibilities and encroach on First Amendment rights. But on the other side, American police have been behaving within the law concerning stop and frisk polices and the use of deadly force. If judges and legislatures change the law, there is every reason to believe that American police will behave in accordance with new regulations, policies, and laws. Until then, because police officers have such important roles in American society and culture, their full understanding of black innocence, black crime, and black poverty is a worthy goal for all concerned individuals and groups.[8]

Ian Ayres and Daniel Markovits suggested in a December 25, 2014, opinion piece in the *Washington Post* that before racially profiled encounters with police can escalate into homicide, in the absence of probable cause for a serious crime, there ought to be rules of engagement for police encounters. Ayres and Markovits propose that officers issue warnings to stop, and then secure warrants for arrests if they are not obeyed. Such measures would check the present situation, where police homicides for attempted stops regarding minor misdemeanors can result in far more drastic punishment than convictions for minor crimes would.[9]

What about the responses of prosecutors, juries, and grand juries to cases of police homicide involving unarmed black victims? Joshua Deahl, writing for *Bloomberg View* cites the Cato Institute's National Police Misconduct Reporting Project's documentation of 4,861 unique reports of misconduct in 2010, including 127 fatalities. In almost all U.S. jurisdictions, police and prosecutors are on the same legal team in their jurisdictions. Deahl reasons that federal prosecution is not a solution because it would require difficult-to-apply charges of civil rights violations based on victims' race or ethnicity. To achieve some distance from the police-prosecutor team loyalty, Deahl proposes permanent special prosecutors, who would be less costly to maintain than ad hoc special prosecutors.[10]

An especially poignant case of police homicide by a white officer against a black suspect involved Jonathan Ferrell, twenty-four, a former Florida A&M football player, who sought help after a car crash. He knocked on the door of the home of a woman who was alone with her infant child and she called 911. When police arrived, Ferrell approached them and was first tasered and then shot dead by Officer Randall Kerrick, age twenty-seven. The Charlotte-Mecklenburg Police Department called the shooting unlawful, but a first grand jury did not indict. A week later, a second grand jury, from which the district attorney had recused himself, did indict Kerrick for voluntary manslaughter.[11]

Cultures change in small unnoticed ways over varied periods of time and then they can change overnight. Violence will not improve the present situation. Apathy and civic incivility add to personal stress and tensions based on racial identities. Peaceful protest and assembly is still protected under the First Amendment. Living with this crisis requires concern, restraint, civility, and moral appeal to basic human rights that fall through the cracks of present U.S. law.

NOTES

PREFACE

1. George Yancy and Naomi Zack, "What 'White Privilege' Really Means." The Stone, Opinionator, *NYTimes*, November 5, 2014, http://opinionator.blogs.nytimes.com/2014/11/05/what-white-privilege-really-means/#more-154773

2. George Yancy and Naomi Zack, "What 'White Privilege' Really Means." The Stone, Opinionator, November 5, 2014, *The New York Times*, Posts, November 6, 2014, Facebook, https://www.facebook.com/nytimes/posts/10150482504744999

3. "Giuliani and Dyson Argue over Violence in Black Communities," *Meet the Press*, NBC, Nov. 24, 2014. http://www.nbcnews.com/storyline/michael-brown-shooting/giuliani-dyson-argue-over-violence-black-communities-n254431. For a transcript see, http://www.realclearpolitics.com/video/2014/11/23/fireworks_giuliani_vs_michael_eric_dyson_white_police_officers_wont_be_there_if_you_werent_killing_each_other_70_of_the_time.html

4. For discussion of the importance of how early on in a chain of criminal justice such homicides have occurred, and a specific suggestion to correct that with a change in police procedure, see: Ian Ayres and Daniel Markovits, "Ending Excessive Police Force Starts with New Rules of Engagement," *The Washington Post*, December 25, 2014, http://www.washingtonpost.com/opinions/ending-excessive-police-force-

starts-with-new-rules-of-*engagement*/2014/12/25/7fa379c0-8a1e-11e4-
a085-34e9b9f09a58_story.html

5. Thanks to Yvette Alex-Assensoh for making this point after reading the manuscript.

6. Oregon, State and County Quickfacts, U.S. Census, http://
quickfacts.census.gov/qfd/states/41000.html

7. See: Blackpast.Org. "The Black Laws of Oregon, 1844-1857,"
http://www.blackpast.org/perspectives/black-laws-oregon-1844-1857
"NAREB (National Association of Real Estate Brokers) Code of Ethics,
"The Oregon History Project," http://www.ohs.org/education/
oregonhistory/historical_records/dspDocument.cfm?doc_ID=
C62459FE-B688-7AC7-1F037E830F143F40

8. The distinction between the lesser day of ordinary life and the
Greater Day goes back to Ovid's *Fasti,* through the medieval *Book of
Days* and the nineteenth century version by Robert Chambers. The passage is from Lawrence's, "The Flying Fish." See: Keith Sagar, *The Art of
D.H. Lawrence*, New York, NY: Cambridge University Press, 1996, pp.
205-230, quote from p. 206.

9. W. E. B. Du Bois, *The Souls of Black Folk*, New York, NY: New
American Library, 1903, p.19.

10. On the lack of independent scientific foundation for social racial
categories, see: Albert Atkin, *The Philosophy of Race*, Oxford, UK: Acumen, 2012; Nina G. Jablonski, *Living Color:The Biological and Social
Meaning of Skin Color*, Oakland, CA: University of California Press,
2012. John Relethford, *The Human Species: An Introduction to Biological Anthropology,* McGraw Hill, 2009-2012; Naomi Zack, *Philosophy of
Science and Race*, New York, NY: Routledge, 2002.

1. WHITE PRIVILEGE, ENTITLEMENTS, AND RIGHTS

1. From Tamir Rice's Autopsy report, Coyahoga County Medical
Examiner's Office, Case Number IN2014-01991, http://media.newsnet5.
com/uploads/Tamir-Rice-Autopsy-Report-121214.pdf

2. See: Elahe Izadi and Peter Holley, "Video Shows Police Officer
Shooting 12-year old Tamir Rice Within Seconds," *Washington Post,*
November 26, 2014, http://www.washingtonpost.com/news/post-nation/
wp/2014/11/26/officials-release-video-names-in-fatal-police-shooting-of-

12-year-old-cleveland-boy/; Brandon Blackwell, "Cleveland Police Officer Shot Tamir Rice Immediately After Leaving Moving Patrol Car,"
Northeast Ohio Media Group, Cleveland.Com, November 26, 2014.
http://www.cleveland.com/metro/index.ssf/2014/11/cleveland_police_
officer_shot_1.html
For the police video of Tamir Rice's shooting, see "Tamir Rice Shooting," *WKY.com*, a Ganer Company, http://www.wkyc.com/story/news/
local/cleveland/2014/11/26/tamir-rice-shooting-video-released/19530745/

3. The official description is: "This act, signed into law by President
Lyndon Johnson on July 2, 1964, prohibited discrimination in public
places, provided for the integration of schools and other public facilities,
and made employment discrimination illegal. This document was the
most sweeping civil rights legislation since Reconstruction." Civil Rights
Act, 1964. *Our Documents*, http://www.ourdocuments.gov/doc.php?
flash=true&doc=97

4. The importance of acknowledging one's own involvement in ongoing racism and processing it or, in George Yancy's words, "tarrying with
it," should not be minimized. See George Yancy, "Whiteness as Insidi-
ous: On the Embedded and Opaque White Racist Self," in Bettina Bergo
and Tracey Nicholls, *"I Don't See Color": Personal and Critical Perspectives on White Privilege*, University Park, PA: Pennsylvania State University Press, 2015, chap. 7. However, such processing and tarrying is
psychological and educational and although it might be a necessary condition for political discourse and action, it cannot take the place of these.

5. Cf. Lewis R. Gordon, "Critical Reflections on Three Popular
Tropes in the Study of Whiteness," in George Yancy, ed., *What White
Looks Like: African-American Philosophers on the Whiteness Questions*,
New York, NY: Routledge, 2004, pp. 173-94. Gordon's critique of the
idea of white privilege in whiteness studies centers on the problem that
whites cannot be expected to give up those privileges that are basic
rights. My approach here, which draws a bright line between privileges
and rights, does not require that whites sacrifice their rights for the sake
of social justice, because rights need to be protected regardless of race.

6. There were many well-received screeds. The classic is probably
Madison Grant, *The Passing of the Great Race: The Racial Basis of European History*, New York, Charles Scribner, 1916, http://www.
jrbooksonline.com/pdf_books/passingofgreatrace.pdf

7. The literature on U.S. ethnicity is vast, but see: Walter Benn Michaels and Stanley Fish, *Our America: Nativism, Nationalism, and Pluralism (Post-Contemporary Interventions)*, Durham,NC: Duke University Press, 1997; David R. Roediger, *Working Toward Whiteness: How America's Immigrants became White*, Cambridge, MA: Basic Books, 2006; Mary C. Waters, *Ethnic Options: Choosing Identities in America*, LA, CA: University of California Press, 1990.

8. Eduardo Bonilla-Silva, "The Invisible Weight of Whiteness: The Racial Grammar of Everyday Life in Contemporary America," *Ethnic and Racial Studies,* 2012, 35:2, 173-194.

9. Leonard Harris, "'Believe It or Not' or the Ku Klux Klan and American Philosophy Exposed," *Proceedings and Addresses of the American Philosophical Association,* vol. 68, no. 5 (May 1995), pp. 133-137.

10. Thanks to Lewis R. Gordon who coined this word in *Bad Faith and Antiblack Racism*, Atlantic Highlands, NJ: Humanities Press, 1995.

11. See Steve Martinot, "Whiteness, Democracy, and the Hegemonic Mind," in Yancy, ed., *White Self-Criticality Beyond Anti-Racism: How Does It Feel to Be a White Problem?*, Lanham, MD: Lexington Books, 2015, pp. 167-188, from p. 183.

12. Ibid. p. 184.

13. See "Equal Protection," *Legal Information Institute*, Cornell School of Law, http://www.law.cornell.edu/wex/equal_protection

14. For a discussion of how standards of mediocracy prevail among whites, which are disrupted by affirmative action, see Lewis R. Gordon, "The Problem with Affirmative Action," Op-Ed, *TruthOut*, August 2011, http://www.s4.brown.edu/us2010/News/inthenews.PDFs/Jul_Aug.2011/us2010news.2011.08.15.truthout.pdf

15. *Gratz v. Bollinger et al.*, (02-512) (2003) is available from: *Find Law* at http://caselaw.lp.findlaw.com/scripts/getcase.pl?court=US&vol=000&invol=02-516

16. Chief Justice Sandra Day O'Connor, who wrote the majority opinion, specified 25 years from the date of ruling. ("The Court expects that 25 years from now, the use of racial preferences will no longer be necessary to further the interest approved today." Opinion, III, B.). Ibid.

17. Bhashkar Mazumder, "Upward Intergenerational Economic Mobility in the United States."*Economic Mobility Project: Upward Mobility Project: An Initiative of The Pew Charitable Trusts* 2008, http://www.

economicmobility.org/assets/pdfs/EMP_ES_Upward_Mobility.pdf; http://www.pewtrusts.org/en/about/news-room/press-releases/2008/05/29/new-study-on-economic-opportunity-finds-that-americans-experience-upward-economic-mobility-but-for-many-the-magnitude-of-their-movement-is-minimal. Consulted November 29, 2014.

18. For a brief summary of this study, see Annie Lowrey, "Big Study Links Good Teachers to Lasting Gain." *New York Times*. January 6, 2012. http://www.nytimes.com/2012/01/06/education/big-study-links-good-teachers-to-lasting-gain.html?pagewanted=all. For the study itself, see Raj Chetty, John N. Friedman, and Jonah E. Rockoff, "The Long-term Impacts of Teachers: Teacher Value-Added and Student Outcomes in Adulthood," Columbia University and NBER. http://obs.rc.fas.harvard.edu/chetty/value_added.html (both consulted November 29, 2014).

19. See Jonathan Kozol, *Savage Inequalities*, New York: Random House, 1991. For an update, see: Michael Busch, Keeping Faith With the Kids: An Interview with Jonathan Kozol," *Huffington Post*, http://www.huffingtonpost.com/michael-busch/poverty-education_b_2013593.html, October 25, 2012.

20. Thomas S. Dee, "The Race Connection: Are Teachers More Effective with Students Who Share Their Ethnicity?" *Education Next*, (Spring 2004), vol. 4, no. 2, http://educationnext.org/the-race-connection/ (Consulted on November 30, 2014). On racism in the classroom, George Yancy writes, "Classrooms are microcosms of the larger social order and reflective of powerful problematic racist stereotypes and assumptions," from George Yancy, *Look, a White!* Philadelphia, PA: Temple University Press, 2012, Chapter 2, "Looking at Whiteness: Subverting White Academic Spaces Through the Pedagogical Perspective of Bell Hooks," pp. 51-81, quote from p. 52.

21. Jason W. Osborne, "Testing Stereotype Threat: Does Anxiety Explain Race and Sex Differences in Achievement?" *Contemporary Educational Psychology*, vol. 26, no. 3 (July 2001), 291–310.

22. Tracie L. Stewart and Nyla R. Branscombe, "The Costs of Privilege and Dividends of Privilege Awareness: The Social Psychology of Confronting Inequality," in Bettina Bergo and Tracey Nicholls, *"I Don't See Color": Personal and Critical Perspectives on White Privilege*, University Park, PA: Pennsylvania State University Press, 2015, chap. 9.

23. See for instance, Marilyn Nissim-Sabat, "Revisioning 'White Privilege'," in Bettina Bergo and Tracey Nicholls, "*I Don't See Color*," chap. 3.

24. On the theme of the pathology of the black family, see: Interviews with Daniel Patrick Moynihan over his career, with a focus on the Moynihan Report, in "New York's Moynihan," *Local Projects for the Museum of the City of New York*, http://www.youtube.com/watch?v=hPxkJZsz4Kc

25. See: "All Bill Information (Except Text) for H.R.3899 - Voting Rights Amendment Act of 2014, 113th Congress (2013-2014)," https://www.congress.gov/bill/113th-congress/house-bill/3899/all-info

26. "Should Photo ID Be Required to Vote?" Debate Club, *US News*. http://www.usnews.com/debate-club/should-photo-id-be-required-to-vote, November 29, 2014.

27. Josh Levs, "Michael Brown's parents address U.N.: 'We need the world to know,'" *CNN*. November 12, 2014, http://www.cnn.com/2014/11/11/us/ferguson-brown-parents-u-n-/. The United Nations Committee Against Torture (CAT) is described by the United Nations Office of the High Commission on Human Rights as "the body of ten independent experts that monitors implementation of the Convention against Torture and Other Cruel, Inhuman or Degrading Treatment or Punishment by its State parties." The United States is one of its members and Felice Gaer, an American, is vice-chairperson of CAT, through December 2015. http://www.ohchr.org/EN/HRBodies/CAT/Pages/CATIndex.aspx

28. Barbara Applebaum, "Flipping the Script. . . And Still a Problem: Staying in the Anxiety of Being a Problem," in Yancy, ed., *White Self-Criticality beyond Anti-Racism*, pp. 1-17, from p. 5.

29. Peggy McIntosh, "White Privilege: Unpacking the Invisible Backpack," 1989. http://www.deanza.edu/faculty/lewisjulie/White%20Priviledge%20Unpacking%20the%20Invisible%20Knapsack.pdf. Accessed November 23, 2014. Many items in this fifty-item "back pack" could be rephrased in an active voice as something that an enlightened-to-white-privilege white person could do, e.g. "1. I will not arrange to spend most of my time in the company of people of my own race."

30. Alison Bailey, "Despising an Identity They Taught Me to Claim," in Chris J. Cuomo and Kim Q. Hall, *Whiteness: Feminist Philosophical Reflections*, Lanham, MD: Rowman and Littlefield, 1999, pp. 85-104, quote from p. 88.

31. Marilyn Nissim-Sabat, "Revisioning 'White Privilege'" in Bergo and Nicholls, *"I Don't See Color,"* chap. 3.

32. Nancy McHugh, "Keeping the Strange Unfamiliar: The Racial Privilege of Dismantling Whiteness, in Yancy, ed., *White Self-Criticality Beyond Anti-Racism,* pp.141-152.

33. Lizette Alvarez and Cara Buckley, "Zimmerman Acquitted in Killing of Treyvon Martin, *NYTimes,* http://www.nytimes.com/2013/07/14/us/george-zimmerman-verdict-trayvon-martin.html?pagewanted=all, accessed July 14, 2014.

34. Zeke J. Miller, "Obama Speaks: Trayvon Martin Could Have Been Me 35 Years Ago," *Swampland,* July 19, 2013. http://swampland.time.com/2013/07/19/obama-speaks-trayvon-martin-could-have-been-me-35-years-ago/#ixzz2ZWdbfsut

35. Regarding Obama's references to car door clicks and suspicion on elevators, George Yancy examined the very same examples of contemporary suspicion of black men in George Yancy, *Black Bodies/White Gazes: The Continuing Significance of Race,* Rowman and Littlefield, 2008. "The Elevator Effect: Black Bodies/White Bodies," chap. 1.

36. Ibid. p. 4.

37. Robin James, "Contort Yourself: Music, Whiteness, and the Politics of Disorientation," in Yancy, ed., *White Self-Criticality Beyond Anti-Racism,* pp.221-238, from p. 223.

38. Samantha Vice, "Politics, Moral Identity and the Limits of White Silence," in George Yancy and Janine Jones, *Pursuing Trayvon Martin: Historical Contexts and Contemporary Manifestations of Racial Dynamics,* Lanham, MD: Lexington Books, 2013, pp. 205-214, from p. 210.

39. Katherine Cooney, "Man Sells Out of Trayvon Martin Gun Range Targets," *Time,* May 14, 2012. http://newsfeed.time.com/2012/05/14/man-sells-out-of-trayvon-martin-gun-range-targets/

40. Josh Levs, "Michael Brown's parents address U.N.: 'We need the world to know,'" *CNN.* November 12, 2014, http://www.cnn.com/2014/11/11/us/ferguson-brown-parents-u-n-/

41. Ben Popken, "Gun Sales Boom on Black Friday," *NBC News,* November 28, 2014, http://www.nbcnews.com/storyline/business-of-the-holidays/gun-sales-boom-black-friday-n259001; James Covert, "Ferguson Protests Influence Black Friday Gun Sales," *New York Post,* December 2, 2014.

42. "Gun Sales Spike Around Ferguson after 3 Days of Riots," *RT*, August 13, 2014, http://rt.com/usa/180084-gun-sales-ferguson-protests/

43. George Yancy and Shannon Sullivan, "White Anxiety and the Futility of Black Hope," The Stone, Opinionator, *NYTimes,* December 5, 2014, http://opinionator.blogs.nytimes.com/2014/12/05/white-anxiety-and-the-futility-of-black-hope/#more-155185

44. Ibid.

45. "Keep Hope Alive with Reverend Jessie Jackson," http://www.keephopealiveradio.com/main.html

46. It's also interesting that years later, Bush was still stung and outraged by West's remark. See Sean Michaels, "George W Bush: Kanye West Attack Was Worst Moment of Presidency," *The Guardian*, November 4, 2010, http://www.theguardian.com/music/2010/nov/04/george-w-bush-kanye-west

47. See George Yancy and Shannon Sullivan, "White Anxiety and the Futility of Black Hope," The Stone, Opinionator, *NYTimes,* December 5, 2014, http://opinionator.blogs.nytimes.com/2014/12/05/white-anxiety-and-the-futility-of-black-hope/#more-155185

48. See Michaels, "George W. Bush."

49. "States of Incarceration: The Global Context," Prison Policy. Org, http://www.prisonpolicy.org/global/

2. BLACK RIGHTS AND POLICE RACIAL PROFILING

1. *Floyd v City of New York*, see: David Floyd, Lalit Clarkson, Deon Dennis and David Ourlicht, individually and on behalf of all others similarly situated, Plaintiffs, -against- The City of New York, Defendant. UNITED STATES DISTRICT COURT SOUTHERN DISTRICT OF NEW YORK Case 1:08-cv-01034-SAS-HBP Document 373, Filed 08/12/13, pp. 6. http://www.nysd.uscourts.gov/cases/show.php?db=special&id=317

2. Official Documents Search System, United Nations, http://www.un.org/en/documents/ods/

3. Thanks to Mark Alfano for making this point.

4. Jim Heitmeyer, "Police Officer's Oath," Law Officer Connect: Public and Law Enforcement Network, 2010. http://connect.lawofficer.com/profiles/blogs/police-officers-oath, consulted December 12, 2012.

5. The International Association of Chiefs of Police, "What is the Law Enforcement Oath of Honor?" http://www.theiacp.org/What-is-the-Law-Enforcement-Oath-of-Honor

6. See: Christopher E. Stone and Heather H. Ward, "Democratic Policing: A Framework for Action," *Policing and Society: An International Journal of Research and Policy*, vol. 10, no. 1, 2000, published online, May 2010, pp. 11-45.

7. Jeremy Ashkenas and Haeyoun Park, "The Race Gap in America's Police Departments," *NYTimes*, September 4, 2014. http://www.nytimes.com/interactive/2014/09/03/us/the-race-gap-in-americas-police-departments.html?_r=0

8. Marc Mauer and Ryan S. King, "Uneven Justice: State Rates of Incarceration by Race and Ethnicity," The Sentencing Project, http://www.sentencingproject.org/doc/publications/rd_stateratesofincbyraceandethnicity.pdf

9. William Y. Chin, "Law and Order and White Power: White Supremacist Infiltration of Law Enforcement and the Need to Eliminate Racism in the Ranks," *LSD* [Lewis and Clark Law School] *Journal* vol. 6, 2013: 30-98, http://www.lsd-journal.net/archives/Volume6/WhiteSupremacists.pdf

10. Richard A. Oppel, Jr. "Sentencing Shift Gives New Leverage to Prosecutors," *NYTimes*, September 25, 2011, http://www.nytimes.com/2011/09/26/us/tough-sentences-help-prosecutors-push-for-plea-bargains.html?pagewanted=all&_r=0

11. There are a number of reasons why accepting a plea bargain is attractive to even innocent defendants: they save money on legal fees, avoid long waits, avoid the risk of being convicted at trial and serving more time for a greater offense, receive a lesser instead of a greater offense on their records. See: NOLO, Law for all, "Defendants' Incentives for Accepting Plea Bargains: Common Reasons Why Defendants Enter into Plea Bargains." http://www.nolo.com/legal-encyclopedia/plea-bargains-defendants-incentives-29732.html

12. NAACP, Criminal Justice Factsheet, http://www.naacp.org/pages/criminal-justice-fact-sheet

13. For a very interesting journalistic account of this disparity and others, see Matt Taibbi with Molly Crabapple, *The Divide: American Injustice in the Age of the Wealth Gap*, New York, NY: Random House, 2014.

14. See endnote 43, below.

15. Timothy Roufa, "How Dangerous Is a Law Enforcement Career?" *About Careers*, http://criminologycareers.about.com/od/Career_Trends/a/Dangers-In-Criminal-Justice-Careers.htm

16. See: John M. Violanti, *Stress Patterns in Police Work: A Longitudinal Study*, National Criminal Justice Reference Service, U.S. 1983; John M. Violanti, *Police Suicide: Epidemic in Blue*, Springfield, IL: Charles C. Thomas, 2007.

17. Sarah Larimer, "Officer who shot 12-year-old Tamir Rice displayed 'dismal' handgun performance in exercise," Post Nation, *The Washington Post*, December 3, 2014. http://www.washingtonpost.com/news/post-nation/wp/2014/12/03/officer-who-shot-12-year-old-tamir-rice-displayed-dismal-handgun-performance-in-exercise/

18. Ibid.

19. United Nations, Preamble, Universal Declaration of Human Rights, 1948, http://www.un.org/en/documents/udhr/

20. See Naomi Zack, "Philosophical Theories of Justice, Inequality, and Racial Inequality," *Graduate Faculty Philosophy Journal*, Special Issue on Race in the History of Philosophy, New School University, 2014, pp. 353-368.

21. United Nations, Preamble, Universal Declaration of Human Rights, 1948, http://www.un.org/en/documents/udhr/

22. United States Constitution, Amendment XIV, http://www.law.cornell.edu/constitution/amendmentxiv

23. Transcript of Civil Rights Act (1964), http://www.ourdocuments.gov/doc.php?flash=true&doc=97&page=transcript

24. Transcript of the Voting Rights Act (1965) http://www.ourdocuments.gov/doc.php?doc=100&page=transcript

25. Public Law 89-236, Oct. 3, 1965, http://library.uwb.edu/guides/USimmigration/79%20stat%20911.pdf

26. U.S. Constitution, Amendment IV, http://www.law.cornell.edu/constitution/amendmentxiv

27. The Library of Congress, "Photographs of Signs Enforcing Racial Discrimination: Documentation by Farm Security Administration-Office of War Information Photographers," Prints and Photographs Reading Room, *The Library of Congress*. http://www.loc.gov/rr/print/list/085_disc.html

28. See "What to Know: Donald Sterling," *KSBH/KHOG-TV*, August 13, 2014. http://www.4029tv.com/national/what-to-know-donald-sterling-scandal/26095640

29. "Hate Crime—Overview," Civil Rights, Federal Bureau of Investigation, http://www.fbi.gov/about-us/investigate/civilrights/hate_crimes/overview, consulted July 19, 2013.

30. "What is a hate crime?" *CBC News*, Canada, June 15, 2011. http://www.cbc.ca/news/canada/story/2011/06/15/f-hate-crimes.html, consulted on July 13, 2013.

31. "FBI Releases 2011 Hate Crime Statistics," National Press Releases, Federal Bureau of Investigation, http://www.fbi.gov/news/pressrel/press-releases/fbi-\releases-2011-hate-crime-statistics December 10, 2012, consulted July 19, 2013. See also, for more up to date information, Stephanie Condon, "FBI Releases Hate Crime Statistics," *CBS News*, Dec. 8, 3014, http://www.cbsnews.com/news/fbi-releases-hate-crime-statistics/

32. Uniform Crime Reports, Federal Bureau of Investigation, http://www.fbi.gov/about-us/cjis/ucr/crime-in-the-u.s/2011/crime-in-the-u.s.-2011/tables/expanded-homicide-data-table-8

33. Spencer Banzhaf, "The Political Economy of Environmental Justice," Weekly Policy Commentary, *Resources for the Future*, May 29, 2009. http://www.rff.org/Publications/WPC/Pages/09_05_25_Political_Economy_of_Environmental_Justice.aspx

34. Darin D. Fredrickson and Raymond P. Siljander, *Racial Profiling*, Springfield, IL: Charles C. Thomas, 2002, NCJRS Library Abstracts, http://www.ncjrs.gov/App/publications/abstract.aspx?ID=195100

35. In support of this kind of reasoning, see for example the comparative likelihood of crime commission, by race, presented by the New Century Foundation in *The Color of Crime: Race, Crime and Justice in America, New Expanded Edition, 2005,* http://www.colorofcrime.com/colorofcrime2005.html

36. "Stop and Frisk Data," Racial Justice, *New York Civil Liberties Union*, http://www.nyclu.org/content/stop-and-frisk-data

37. New York City, NY, Census Gov Quick Facts, http://quickfacts.census.gov/qfd/states/36/3651000.html

38. The Prison Project, "Incarceration Rates by Race and Ethnicity, 2010,http://www.prisonpolicy.org/graphs/raceinc.html

39. See: "strict scrutiny," Legal Information Institute, Cornell University Law School, http://www.law.cornell.edu/wex/strict_scrutiny

40. *Floyd v City of New York*, see: David Floyd, Lalit Clarkson, Deon Dennis and David Ourlicht, individually and on behalf of all others similarly situated, Plaintiffs, -against- The City of New York, Defendant. UNITED STATES DISTRICT COURT SOUTHERN DISTRICT OF NEW YORK Case 1:08-cv-01034-SAS-HBP Document 373, Filed 08/12/13, pp. 5-6. http://www.nysd.uscourts.gov/cases/show.php?db=special&id=317

41. Ibid. p. 9.

42. Ibid. pp. 13-18.

43. Brigitt Keller,"Stop and Frisk: Legal and Political Maneuvering Delays Justice," National Lawyers Guild, *Guild Notes*, Winter 2013. http://connection.ebscohost.com/c/articles/94720845/stop-frisk-legal-political-maneuvering-delays-justice

44. James Q. Wilson and George L. Kelling, "Broken Windows: The Police and Neighborhood Safety." *Atlantic Monthly*, March 1982, http://www.manhattan-institute.org/pdf/_atlantic_monthly-broken_windows.pdf

45. Michael Weisser, "It's Clear Violent Crime Is Decreasing, But Less Clear Why," http://www.huffingtonpost.com/mike-weisser/violent-crime-cities_b_4760996.html

46. Bernard E. Harcourt and Jens Ludwig, "Broken Windows: New Evidence from New York City and a Five-City Social Experiment," *University of Chicago Law Review*, 73, June 2005, http://www.law.uchicago.edu/files/files/93-beh-jl-windows.pdf

47. Andrew Jerell Jones, "Bottom of Form: New York Allowed To Legally Abandon 'Stop-and-Frisk' Nonsense," First Look. Org. https://firstlook.org/theintercept/2014/10/31/new-york-city-moves-forward-changing-stop-frisk-nonsense/

48. Caroline Bankoff, "Police Union Encourages Cops to Ban de Blasio from Their Funerals," *Daily Intelligencer*, December 13, 2014. http://nymag.com/daily/intelligencer/2014/12/pba-encourages-cops-to-ban-mayor-from-funerals.html

49. Ryan Devereaux, " De Blasio Administration Continues Attacks on Press Over NYPD Spying, Channeling Bloomberg," *FirstLook.Org*, October 8, 2014. https://firstlook.org/theintercept/2014/10/08/

channeling-bloomberg-de-blasio-administration-continues-attacks-press-nypd-spying/

50. See Falguni A. Sheth, "Muslim Immigrants in Post 9-11 American Politics: The 'Exception' Population as an Intrinsic Element of American Liberalism," in Linda Martin Alcoff and Mariana Ortega, eds., *Constructing the Nation: A Race and Nationalism Reader*, Albany, NY: SUNY Press, 2009, pp. 103-130.

51. Laura Sullivan, "Obama Administration Reveals New Limits on Racial Profiling," *NPR News*, December 8, 2017. http://www.npr.org/blogs/thetwo-way/2014/12/08/369388099/obama-administration-unveils-new-ban-on-racial-profiling

52. "S.1038 - End Racial Profiling Act of 2013, 113th Congress (2013-2014)," Congress.gov, https://www.congress.gov/bill/113th-congress/senate-bill/1038

53. Sophia Kerby, "The Top 10 Most Startling Facts About People of Color and Criminal Justice in the United States: A Look at the Racial Disparities Inherent in Our Nation's Criminal-Justice System," *Center for American Progress*, March 13, 2013. http://www.americanprogress.org/issues/race/news/2012/03/13/11351/the-top-10-most-startling-facts-about-people-of-color-and-criminal-justice-in-the-united-states/

54. Rod K. Brunson and Jody Miller, "Young Black Men and Urban Policing in the United States," *British Journal of Criminology*, vol. 46, no. 4 (July 2006), pp. 613-640 http://www.jstor.org/stable/23639456, p. 616.

55. *Floyd v. The City of New York*, p. 95, from Charles Blow, "The Whole System Failed Trayvon Martin," *NYTimes*, July 15, 2013.

56. For the full facts of that encounter, from different perspectives, see George Yancy and Janine Jones, *Pursuing Trayvon Martin: Historical Contexts and Contemporary Manifestations of Racial Dynamics*, Lanham, MD: Lexington Books, 2013, Introduction, pp. 1-24. See also the discussion of Trayvon Martin and George Zimmerman in chapter 3.

57. Genesis, King James Version (Meridian 1974); William Blackstone, Commentaries °358, quoted by Alexander Volokh in "Guilty Men," *University of Pennsylvania Law Review* 173 (1997), http://www2.law.ucla.edu/volokh/guilty.htm#1. Volokh's extremely erudite and comprehensive intellectual history of the number of guilty men permitted to

go unpunished to save the innocent has much surprising scholarly and anecdotal information.

58. George Yancy, "Walking While Black in the White Gaze," The Stone, Opinionator, *NYTimes*, September 1, 2013. http://opinionator. blogs.nytimes.com/2013/09/01/walking-while-black-in-the-white-gaze/?_r=0

59. Amanda Geller, Jeffrey Fagan, Tom Tyler, and Bruce G. Link, "Aggressive Policing and the Mental Health of Young Urban Men," *American Journal of Public Health*, December 2014, vol. 104, no. 12, pp. 2321-2327. http://ajph.aphapublications.org/doi/abs/10.2105/AJPH.2014. 302046

60. From *Terry v. Ohio*, 392 U.S. 1, 16–17 (1968), quoted as an epigraph to the decision in *Floyd v. City of New York*, see: David Floyd, Lalit Clarkson, Deon Dennis and David Ourlicht, individually and on behalf of all others similarly situated, Plaintiffs, -against- The City of New York, Defendant. UNITED STATES DISTRICT COURT SOUTHERN DISTRICT OF NEW YORK Case 1:08-cv-01034-SAS-HBP Document 373, Filed 08/12/13, p.1 http://www.nysd.uscourts.gov/cases/show.php?db=special&id=317

61. Rod K. Brunson and Jody Miller, "Young Black Men and Urban Policing in the United States," *British Journal of Criminology*, vol. 46, no. 4 (July 2006), pp. 613-640. http://www.jstor.org/stable/23639456

62. Howard M. Wasserman, "Moral Panics and Body Cameras," *Washington University Law Review* Commentaries, November 18, 2014, http://openscholarship.wustl.edu/

63. On the Rodney King case, see: Seth Mydans, "Los Angeles Policemen Acquitted in Taped Beating," *NYTimes*, April 30, 1992. http://www. nytimes.com/learning/general/onthisday/big/0429.html. See chapter 3 for discussion of Oscar Grant's case.

3. BLACK INJUSTICE AND POLICE HOMICIDE

1. Lawrence Kobilinsky, forensics expert and Chair of the Department of Sciences at the John Jay College of Criminal Justice in New York City, commenting on the death of Tamir Rice. Kobilinsky is making the point that homicide has two meanings in law: death of one human being by another; criminal death of one human being by another. See "Homi-

cide Definition," *FindLaw*, http://criminal.findlaw.com/criminal-charges/homicide-definition.html; *Crimesider* Staff, "Autopsy calls Tamir Rice shooting death a homicide," *CBS News/AP*, December 12, 2014, http://www.cbsnews.com/news/medical-examiner-rules-tamir-rices-death-a-homicide/

2. Jaeah Lee, "Exactly How Often Do Police Shoot Unarmed Black Men?: The killing in Ferguson was one of many such cases. Here's what the data reveals." *Mother Jones*, August 15, 2014, http://www.motherjones.com/politics/2014/08/police-shootings-michael-brown-ferguson-black-men

3. Kevin Johnson, Meghan Hoyer and Brad Heath, "Local Police Involved in 400 Killings a Year," *USA TODAY*, August 15, 2014. http://www.usatoday.com/story/news/nation/2014/08/14/police-killings-data/14060357/

4. "Operation Ghetto Storm: 2012 Annual Report on the Extrajudicial Killing of 313 Black People," *Malcolm X Grassroots Movement*, May 2013. http://mxgm.org/operation-ghetto-storm-2012-annual-report-on-the-extrajudicial-killing-of-313-black-people/

5. Katie Sanders, "An unarmed black person is shot 'every 28 hours,' says Marc Lamont Hill," Punditfact, *Tampa Bay Times*, December 18, 2014, http://www.politifact.com/punditfact/statements/2014/aug/26/marc-lamont-hill/unarmed-black-person-shot-every-28-hours-says-ma/

6. Naomi Zack, *The Ethics and Mores of Race: Equality After the History of Philosophy*, Lanham, MD: Rowman and Littlefield, 2011 and 2015.

7. John Rawls, *A Theory of Justice*, Chicago, IL: University of Chicago Press, 1971, pp. 19-20.

8. Ibid. p. 20.

9. Rawls was not a philosopher of science and did not relate his theory of justice to theories in other fields. However, my basic point that his theory of justice is a theory because it provides an explanation of existing beliefs from which other beliefs can be derived, should not be controversial. For an overview of explanation in science and related sources, see James Woodward, "Scientific Explanation," *Stanford Encyclopedia of Philosophy* (Winter 2014 Edition), Edward N. Zalta (ed.), forthcoming. http://plato.stanford.edu/archives/win2014/entries/scientific-explanation/

10. See George Yancy's interview of Charles Mills, "Lost in Rawls-land" The Stone, Opinionator, *NY Times*, November 16, 2014. http://opinionator.blogs.nytimes.com/category/the-stone/; see also, Charles W. Mills, "Rawls on Race/Race in Rawls, *The Southern Journal of Philosophy (2009)* vol. XLVII, pp. 160-185, quote from p. 161. http://www.havenscenter.wisc.edu/files/Mills-Rawls%20on%20Race.pdf, consulted on Nov. 28, 2014.

11. Mills, "Lost in Rawlsland."

12. Giorgio Agamben, Kevin Attell trans. *The State of Exception*, Chicago, IL: University of Chicago Press, 2005; Amartya Sen, *The Idea of Justice*, Cambridge, MA: Harvard University Press, 2009.

13. Sally Haslanger, "Social Meaning and Philosophic Method," *Proceedings and Addresses of the American Philosophical Association*, vol. 88, November 2014, pp. 16-30.

14. Lucius Outlaw, "Africana Philosophy," in *The Stanford Encyclopedia of Philosophy*, October, 2010, http://plato.stanford.edu/entries/africana/, cited by Janine Jones, "Can We Imagine *This* Happening to a White Boy," in Yancy and Jones, eds., *Pursuing Trayvon Martin*, p. 142, full citation n. 22. (quote from sec. 2).

15. See Jacques Maritain, "The Grounds for an International Declaration of Human Rights (1947)," in Micheline Ishay, ed., *The Human Rights Reader*, New York, NY: Routledge, pp. 2-6.

16. See: United Nations, "Universal Declaration of Human Rights," http://www.un.org/en/documents/udhr/index.shtml#ap

17. Ibid.

18. Mills, "Rawls on Race/Race in Rawls, *Southern Journal of Philosophy*. Special Issue: *Spindel Supplement: Race, Racism, and Liberalism in the 21st Century*, vol. 47, no. S1 (Spring 2009): pp. 161–184.

19. See for instance, Tommy Shelby, "Justice, Deviance, and the Dark Ghetto," *Philosophy & Public Affairs*, vol. 35, no. 2 (Spring 2007): pp. 126–160. In this article, Shelby begins: "Throughout I will stress the importance of assessing the moral status of the ghetto poor's conduct, within nonideal political theory, that undeveloped part of the theory of justice that specifies how we should respond to or rectify injustice," p. 127.

20. For an introduction to The Theory of Applicative Justice, see Naomi Zack, "Racial Inequality and a Theory of Applicative Justice," *APA*

Newsletter on Philosophy and the Black Experience, The American Philosophical Association, vol. 13, no. 1 (Fall 2013): pp. 6-11.

21. Michelle Alexander, *The New Jim Crow: Mass Incarceration in the Age of Colorblindness*, New York, NY: The New Press, Kindle Edition, 2012, p. 200. Cited by Janine Jones in "Can We Imagine *This* Happening to a White Boy," in Yancy and Jones, eds. *Pursuing Trayvon Martin*, p. 142, full citation n. 22.

22. Janine Jones, "Can We Imagine *This* Happening to a White Boy," in George Yancy and Janine Jones, eds., *Pursuing Trayvon Martin: Historical Contexts and Contemporary Manifestations of Racial Dynamics*, Lanham, MD: Lexington Books, 2013, pp. 141-154. quote from p. 141. The quote of Wills by Jones is from Vanessa Wills, "What Are Your Doing Around Here?: Trayvon Martin and the Logic of Black Guilt," in ibid. 225-236, quote from p. 230.

23. Vanessa Wills, "What Are Your Doing Around Here?: Trayvon Martin and the Logic of Black Guilt," in ibid. pp. 225-236, quote from p. 230.

24. Brian A. Reaves, "Census of State and Local Law Enforcement Agencies," *Bureau of Justice Statistics*, U.S. Department of Justice, http://bjs.ojp.usdoj.gov/content/pub/pdf/csllea08.pdf

25. See U.S. Census, Vintage 2008 data, http://www.census.gov/popest/data/historical/2000s/vintage_2008/

26. Many sources concur on that figure. See for example, Mark Hugo Lopez and Paul Taylor, "Dissecting the 2008 Electorate: Most Diverse in US History," Pew Research Hispanic Trends Project, and http://www.pewhispanic.org/2009/04/30/dissecting-the-2008-electorate-most-diverse-in-us-history/ and Sean Trende, "The Case of the Missing White Voters," *Real Clear Politics*, November 8, 2012, http://www.realclearpolitics.com/articles/2012/11/08/the_case_of_the_missing_white_voters_116106-2.html

27. However, it has been claimed that Zimmerman did not present a "stand your ground" defense, because he claimed that he was restrained, with retreat not possible for him, at the time he shot Martin. Jacob Sullum, "Sorry, the Zimmerman Case Still has nothing to do with 'Stand Your Ground,'" July 13, 2013. Hit and Run Blog, *Reason.Com*, http://reason.com/blog/2013/07/14/sorry-the-zimmerman-case-still-has-nothi (consulted July 20, 2013).

28. *CNN* US, "Trayvon Martin Shooting Fast Facts," *CNN Library*, http://www.cnn.com/2013/06/05/us/trayvon-martin-shooting-fast-facts, July 13, 2013.

29. *State of Florida vs. George Zimmerman*, Circuit Court of the Eighteenth Judicial Circuit, in and for Seminole County, Florida, Case No.: 2012 CF 1083 AXXX, http://media.cmgdigital.com/shared/news/documents/2013/07/12/jury_instructions_1.pdf

30. The reason for the 911 operator's instruction did not emerge. It's possible that the operator did not think Zimmerman was sufficiently trained or experienced to evaluate the danger posed by Martin and that if he rushed in, unnecessary violence could result—which was what happened. Or, the operator may have been concerned for Zimmerman's safety. A more experienced police officer might have been able to "socially decode" Martin, based on his appearance and behavior and reached a conclusion that no intervention was necessary. For a discussion of social decoding by experienced police personnel, see David Wasserman, "Racial Generalizations and Police Discretion," in John Kleinig, ed., *Handled with Discretion: Ethical Issues in Police Decision Making*, Lanham, MD: Rowman and Littlefield, 1996, pp. 115-130, esp. pp. 126 ff.

31. I am grateful to Allen Faigen, a student in my Fall 2013 Philosophy of Race course at the University of Oregon, for bringing my attention to the need to specify antecedent readiness in this sense, before the event of actually using the gun. As for Zimmerman's self-image as heroic, he was reported to have come out of hiding nine days after his acquittal to rescue a family of four from a burning truck crash. (Danielle Cadette, *Huffington Post*: Black Voices, July 22, 2013, http://www.huffingtonpost.com/2013/07/22/george-zimmerman-truck-accident-rescue_n_3635628.html) However, it was subsequently reported that a friend in the local sheriff's office had called Zimmerman right after the crash to suggest that he would have an opportunity to appear heroic if he showed up. (See Dog Gone, "George Zimmerman's Heroic Car Crash Rescue Appears to be a Fraud—Updated," July 25, 2013. *IVN*, http://ivn.us/2013/07/25/george-zimmermans-heroic-car-crash-rescue-appears-to-be-a-fraud/

32. Adam Aigner-Treworgy, "Petitions Gain Signatures after Zimmerman Verdict,"CNN White House Producer, *CNN Politics,* http://politicalticker.blogs.cnn.com/2013/07/15/white-house-petitions-gain-signatures-after-zimmerman-verdict/

33. Steph Solis, Molly Vorwerck, Jordan Friedman, and John Bacon, "Justice for Trayvon Rallies in 100 Cities Across the US.," *USA TODAY* July 20, 2013. http://www.usatoday.com/story/news/nation/2013/07/20/justice-trayvon-martin-vigils-zimmerman/2571025/

34. The NAACP asked the attorney general to pursue action against Zimmerman on the grounds that he violated Martin's civil rights, see: Terry Shropshire, "NAACP Demand Department of Justice Prosecute George Zimmerman for Hate Crime," *RollingOut*, July 15, 2013. http://rollingout.com/criminal-behavior/naacp-demands-department-of-justice-prosecute-george-zimmerman-for-hate-crime/

35. Arthur Weinreb, "Did George Zimmerman Stalk Trayvon Martin? Unlawful Pursuit Law in Florida, " *Decoded Science*, July 23, 2013, http://www.decodedscience.com/did-george-zimmerman-stalk-trayvon-martin-unlawful-pursuit-law-in-florida/33899/2

36. See: Howard Cohen, "Police Discretion and Police Objectivity," in Kleinig, ed., *Handled with Discretion*, pp. 96-106.

37. See "8 (Great?) Hunting-Humans-For-Sport Movies." *Go*, http://www.omaha.com/go/great-hunting-humans-for-sport-movies/article_444aca49-0896-54e3-bf88-799c68199e46.html

38. See "Lynching," *Black History Pages*, http://blackhistorypages.com/Lynching/, consulted December 10, 2014.

39. Brian Miller, "Fruitvale Station," *Seattle Weekly*, June 23, 2013. http://www.imdb.com/title/tt2334649/

40. Aisha Harris, "How Accurate Is Fruitvale Station?" Browbeat, *Slate's Culture Blog*, July 13, 2013, http://www.slate.com/blogs/browbeat/2013/07/12/fruitvale_station_true_story_fact_and_fiction_in_movie_about_bart_train.html

41. Jack Leonard, "Former Bart Officer Convicted of Involuntary Manslaughter," *Los Angeles Times* July 8, 2010, http://www.sfexaminer.com/sanfrancisco/johannes-mehserle-four-others-cleared-in-bart-police-brutality-trial/Content?oid=2187307

42. Will Reisman, "Johannes Mehserle, Four Others Cleared in BART Police Brutality Trial," *The Examiner*, December 2, 2011. http://www.sfexaminer.com/sanfrancisco/johannes-mehserle-four-others-cleared-in-bart-police-brutality-trial/Content?oid=2187307

43. Rachel Clarke and Christopher Lett, "What Happened When Michael Brown Met Officer Darren Wilson," *CNN News*, November 11,

2014, http://www.cnn.com/interactive/2014/08/us/ferguson-brown-timeline/

44. Steven Payne, "St. Louis County District Attorney Bob McCulloch Knew Witnesses Were Lying," Ferguson Grand Jury Project, *Daily KOS*, December 20, 2014, http://www.dailykos.com/blog/Ferguson%20Grand%20Jury%20Investigation%20Project/

45. Eyda Peralta and Krishnadev Calamur, "Ferguson Documents: How the Grand Jury Reached a Decision," The Two-Way, *NPR.ORG*, November 25, 2014, http://www.npr.org/blogs/thetwo-way/2014/11/25/366507379/ferguson-docs-how-the-grand-jury-reached-a-decision

46. *United States v. Williams*, U.S. Supreme Court, (90-1972), 504 U.S. 36 (1992), Legal Information Institute, Cornell University Law School, http://www.law.cornell.edu/supct/html/90-1972.ZO.html

47. Ibid. cited by Jud Lugum, in "Justice Scalia Explains What Was Wrong with The Ferguson Grand Jury," *Think Progress.Org.* November 26, 2011. http://thinkprogress.org/justice/2014/11/26/3597322/justice-scalia-explains-what-was-wrong-with-the-ferguson-grand-jury/

48. See footnotes 49 and 50, below.

49. Barry Paddock, Rocco Parascandolla, and Corky Siemaszko, "HOMICIDE: Medical examiner says NYPD Chokehold Killed Staten Island Dad Eric Garner," *New York Daily News*, August 2, 2014, http://www.nydailynews.com/new-york/nyc-crime/eric-garner-death-ruled-homicide-medical-examiner-article-1.1888808

50. Nadine DeNinno, "Eric Garner Death By NYPD Chokehold: Second Video Showing EMT's Not Helping Man Raises More Questions," *International Business Times*, July, 22, 2014. http://www.ibtimes.com/eric-garner-death-nypd-chokehold-second-video-showing-emts-not-helping-man-raises-more-1635388

51. J. David Goodman and Al Baker, "Wave of Protests After Grand Jury Doesn't Indict Officer in Eric Garner Chokehold Case," *NYTimes,* December 3, 2014, http://www.nytimes.com/2014/12/04/nyregion/grand-jury-said-to-bring-no-charges-in-staten-island-chokehold-death-of-eric-garner.html

52. Harry Enten, "The Grand Jury in the Eric Garner Case Was Especially Unlikely to Indict," DataLab, *FiveThirtyEight.Com,* December 3, 2014. http://fivethirtyeight.com/datalab/eric-garner-chokehold-staten-island-grand-jury-indict/

53. James C. McKinley Jr. and Al Baker, "Grand Jury System, with Exceptions, Favors the Police in Fatalities" *NYTimes*, December 7, 2014, http://www.nytimes.com/2014/12/08/nyregion/grand-juries-seldom-charge-police-officers-in-fatal-actions.html?_r=0. McKinley and Baker derive their figures from research by Philip M. Stinson, criminologist at Bowling Green State University, http://works.bepress.com/philip_stinson/

54. *Gramme v. Connor,* 490 U.S. 389 (1989).

55. Ibid. pp. 396-397.

56. See Mary Reichard, "Lethal Force in Ferguson and Beyond," December 1, 2014, *World*, Real Matters/WNG.Org, http://www.worldmag.com/2014/12/lethal_force_in_ferguson_and_beyond/

57. *Plumhoff et al. v. Rickard*, U.S. Supreme Court, October Term, 2013, http://www.supremecourt.gov/opinions/13pdf/12-1117_1bn5.pdf

58. *Tennessee v. Garner*, 471 U.S. 1 (1985), FindLaw, pp. 7-12. http://caselaw.lp.findlaw.com/scripts/getcase.pl?court=US&vol=471&invol=1

59. *Terry v. Ohio.* 392 I/S/ 1(1968), No 67. http://scholar.google.com/scholar_case?case=17773604035873288886&q=terry+v.+ohio,+us+supreme+court&hl=en&as_sdt=3,38

60. Ibid. p. 16

61. Ibid. p. 19

62. Ibid. p. 21.

63. Ibid. p. 22.

64. Ibid. p. 27.

65. James Hill, "Milwaukee Police Officer Not Charged in Fatal Shooting," December 22, 2014, *ABC News*, http://abcnews.go.com/US/milwaukee-police-officer-charged-fatal-shooting/story?id=27767944

66. Elizabeth A Phelps, "Race, Behavior, and the Brain: The Role of Neuroimaging in Understanding Complex Social Behaviors," *Political Psychology*, vol. 24, no. 4, Special Issue: *Neuroscientific Contributions to Political Psychology* (December 2003): pp. 747-758

CONCLUSION

1. Donald Byrne, *Catholic Journals US: Reflections on Faith and Culture*, August 4, 2011, http://www.catholicjournal.us/2011/08/04/if-you-want-peace-work-for-justice/

2. For news accounts of these events, see: Benjamin Mueller and Al Baker, "2 N.Y.P.D. Officers Killed in Brooklyn Ambush; Suspect Commits Suicide," *NYTimes*, December 20, 2014, http://www.nytimes.com/2014/12/21/nyregion/two-police-officers-shot-in-their-patrol-car-in-brooklyn.html; Pervaiz Shallwani, "NYPD Shooting Suspect Referenced Garner, Brown Cases Officers Were 'Targeted for Their Uniform,' Police Commissioner Says," *Wall Street Journal*, Dec. 21, 2014, http://www.wsj.com/articles/two-nypd-officers-shot-in-patrol-car-1419112127; J. David Goodman, "New York Police Try to Trace History of Violent Day," *NYTimes*, December 21, 2014, http://www.nytimes.com/2014/12/21/nyregion/police-combing-through-shooting-suspects-arrest-history-and-violent-day.html?_r=0NYT; Yamiche Alcindor and John Bacon, "NYC Mourns Officers as Rift Widens between Union, Mayor," *USA TODAY*, December 21, 2014, http://www.usatoday.com/news/; Marc Santora and J. David Goodman, "After Shooting, a City Mourns the Deaths of Two Officers," *NYT Now*, December 21, 2014, http://www.nytimes.com/2014/12/22/nyregion/a-divided-city-mourns-the-deaths-of-two-officers.html; Dan Riehl, "Al Sharpton Denounces NYC Cop Killings, Reports Death Threats Against Himself," *BREITBART*, December 21, 2014, http://www.breitbart.com/big-journalism/2014/12/21/al-sharpton-denounces-nyc-cop-killings-reports-death-threats-against-himself/; Kate Sheppard, "Rudy Giuliani Accuses Obama, Black Leaders Of Stoking 'Anti-Police Hatred,'" *Huffington Post, Politics*, December 21, 2014, http://www.huffingtonpost.com/2014/12/21/giuliani-new-york-police-obama_n_6362724.html

3. On the subject of the importance of public memorials and collective remembering for harms done to African Americans, see, Al Frankowski, *Post-Racial Violence, Mourning, and the Limits of Memorialization*, Lanham, MD: Lexington Books, forthcoming.

4. Marc Santora, "Mayor de Blasio Calls for Suspension of Protests," *NYTimes*, December 22, 2014. http://www.nytimes.com/2014/12/23/nyregion/mayor-bill-de-blasio-nypd-officers-shooting.html; Patrick Lynch's vulgar political rhetoric is directly quoted in Tina Moore, Rocco

Parascandola, and Thomas Tracy, "Patrolmen's Benevolent Association President Patrick Lynch blasts de Blasio, says he is 'running a f---ing revolution'" *New York Daily News*, December 18, 2014. http://www. nydailynews.com/news/politics/pba-president-blasts-de-blasio-runs-revolution-article-1.2050551; For argument about the harms of racial profiling, see Annabelle Lever, "Why Racial Profiling is Hard to Justify: A Response to Risse and Zeckhauser," *Philosophy and Public Affairs*, 33(1), 2005: 94–110.

5. "List of Police Television Drama," *Wikipedia*, http://en.wikipedia.org/wiki/List_of_police_television_dramas

6. Carlos Fields, "Award-Winning Community Policing Strategies, 1999-2006, A Report for the International Association of Chiefs of Police," Community Policing Committee, U.S. Department of Justice, COPS Office Community Policing, http://ric-zai-inc.com/Publications/cops-w0451-pub.pdf

7. Ronald Bailey, "Don't Be Terrorized," *Reason.Com*, August 11, 2006. http://reason.com/archives/2006/08/11/dont-be-terrorized

8. Thanks to Kwandwo Assensoh for stressing this point in relation to general ways in which those who are motivated by ideologies may not fully understand their own actions.

9. Ian Ayres and Daniel Markovits, "Ending Excessive Police Force Starts With New Rules of Engagement," *Washington Post*, December 25, 2014, http://www.washingtonpost.com/opinions/ending-excessive-police-force-starts-with-new-rules-of-engagement/2014/12/25/7fa379c0-8ale-11e4-a085-34e9b9f09a58_story.html.

10. Joshua Daehl, "Police Killings Call for New Kind of Prosecutor," *Bloomberg View*, December 4, 2014, http://www.bloombergview.com/articles/2014-12-04/police-killings-call-for-new-kind-of-prosecutor

11. "Jonathan Ferrell Killed: Man Shot in North Carolina Was A Former FAMU Football Player," *AP*, November 13, 2013. *Huffington Post, Crime*, http://www.huffingtonpost.com/2013/09/15/jonathanferrell-killed_n_3931282.html; Eliott C. McLaughlin, "2nd grand jury indicts officer in shooting of ex-FAMU football player," *CNN*, January 28, 2014. http://www.cnn.com/2014/01/27/us/north-carolina-police-shooting/

SELECT BIBLIOGRAPHY

Internet addresses under the sections below were consulted November-December 2014

COURT CASES

Floyd et al. v. The City of New York et. al. 08-civ. 1034 (AT) (2014)
Graham v. Connor, 490 U.S. 389 (1989)
Gratz v. Bollinger, 539 U.S. 244 (2003)
Grutter v. Bollinger et al., 539 U.S. 306 (2003)
Plumhoff et al. v. Rickard, U.S. Supreme Court, 12-1117. October Term, 2013
State of Florida vs. George Zimmerman, Circuit Court of the Eighteenth Judicial Circuit, in and for Seminole County, Florida, Case No.: 2012 CF 1083 AXXX
Tennessee v. Garner, 471 U.S. 1 (1985)
Terry v. Ohio. 392 US/1(1968), No 67
United States v. Williams, U.S. Supreme Court, 504 U.S. 36 (1992)

INTERVIEWS

Michael Busch, "Keeping Faith with the Kids: An Interview with Jonathan Kozol," *Huffington Post,* www.huffingtonpost.com/michael-busch/poverty-education_b_2013593.html, October 25, 2012.
George Yancy and Charles Mills, "Lost in Rawlsland," The Stone, Opinionator, *NYTimes* http://opinionator.blogs.nytimes.com/author/charles-mills/?_r=0 November 16, 2014
George Yancy and Shannon Sullivan, "White Anxiety and the Futility of Black Hope," The Stone, Opinionator, *NYTimes,* December 5, 2014, http://opinionator.blogs.

nytimes.com/2014/12/05/white-anxiety-and-the-futility-of-black-hope/#more-155185

George Yancy and Naomi Zack, "What 'White Privilege Really Means," The Stone, Opinionator, NYTimes, November 5, 2015 http://opinionator.blogs.nytimes.com/2014/11/05/what-white-privilege-really-means/#more-154773

VIDEOS

Giuliani, Rudy and Michael Eric Dyson, "Giuliani and Dyson Argue over Violence in Black Communities," Meet the Press, NBC, November 24, 2014. http://www.nbcnews.com/storyline/michael-brown-shooting/giuliani-dyson-argue-over-violence-black-communities-n254431. For a transcript see, http://www.realclearpolitics.com/video/2014/11/23/fireworks_giuliani_vs_michael_eric_dyson_white_police_officers_wont_be_there_if_you_werent_killing_each_other_70_of_the_time.html

Izadi, Elahe and Peter Holley, "Video Shows Police Officer Shooting 12-year old Tamir Rice Within Seconds," Washington Post, November 26, 2014, Brandon Blackwell, "Cleveland police officer shot Tamir Rice immediately after leaving moving patrol car," Northeast Ohio Media Group, cleveland.com, November 26, 2014. http://www.cleveland.com/metro/index.ssf/2014/11/cleveland_police_officer_shot_1.html. For the police video of Tamir Rice's shooting, see "Tamir Rice Shooting," WKY.com, a Ganer Company, http://www.wkyc.com/story/news/local/cleveland/2014/11/26/tamir-rice-shooting-video-released/19530745/

BOOKS

Agamben, Giorgio, Kevin Attell, trans. The State of Exception, Chicago, IL: University of Chicago Press, 2005

Atkin, Albert, The Philosophy of Race, Oxford, UK: Acumen, 2012

Bergo, Bettina and Tracey Nicholls, "I Don't See Color": Personal and Critical Perspectives on White Privilege, University Park, PA: Pennsylvania State University Press, 2015

Cuomo, Chris J. and Kim Q. Hall, Whiteness: Feminist Philosophical Reflections, Lanham, MD: Rowman and Littlefield, 1999

Du Bois, W.E.B., The Souls of Black Folk, New York, NY: New American Library, 1903

Grant, Madison, The Passing of the Great Race: The Racial Basis of European History, New York, Charles Scribner, 1916, http://www.jrbooksonline.com/pdf_books/passingofgreatrace.pdf

Ishay, Micheline ed. The Human Rights Reader, New York, NY: Routledge, 2007

Jablonski, Nina G., Living Color: The Biological and Social Meaning of Skin Color, Oakland, CA: University of California Press, 2012

Kleinig John,ed., Handled with Discretion: Ethical Issues in Police Decision Making, Lanham, MD: Rowman & Littlefield, 1996

Kozol, Jonathon, Savage Inequalities, New York: Random House, 1991

Sagar, Keith, *The Art of D.H. Lawrence*, New York, NY: Cambridge University Press, 1996

Rawls, John, *A Theory of Justice*, Chicago, IL: University of Chicago Press, 1971

Relethford, John, *The Human Species: An Introduction to Biological Anthropology*, McGraw Hill, 2009-2012

Roediger, David R., *Working Toward Whiteness: How America's Immigrants Became White*, Cambridge, MA: Basic Books, 2006

Sen, Amartya, *The Idea of Justice*, Cambridge, MA: Harvard University Press, 2009

Yancy, George, and Janine Jones, eds., *Pursuing Trayvon Martin: Historical Contexts and Contemporary Manifestations of Racial Dynamics*, Lanham, MD: Lexington Books, 2013

Yancy, George ed., *White Self-Criticality Beyond Anti-Racism: How Does It Feel to Be a White Problem?* Lanham, MD: Lexington Books, 2014

_____, *Look, a White!* Philadephia, PA: Temple University Press, 2012.

_____, *What White Looks Like: African-American Philosophers on the Whiteness Questions*, New York, NY: Routledge, 2004

Zack, Naomi, *The Ethics and Mores of Race: Equality After the History of Philosophy*, Lanham, MD: Rowman and Littlefield, 2011 and 2015.

_____, *Philosophy of Science and Race*, New York, NY: Routledge, 2002

ARTICLES AND REPORTS

Ayres, Ian and Daniel Markovits, "Ending Excessive Police Force Starts with New Rules of Engagement," *The Washington Post*, December 25, 2014, http://www.washingtonpost.com/opinions/ending-excessive-police-force-starts-with-new-rules-of-engagement/2014/12/25/7fa379c0-8a1e-11e4-a085-34e9b9f09a58_story.html

Bhashkar, Mazumder, "Upward Intergenerational Economic Mobility in the United States."
Economic Mobility Project; Upward Mobility Project: An Initiative of The Pew Charitable Trusts 2008.
http://www.economicmobility.org/assets/pdfs/EMP_ES_Upward_Mobility.pdf
http://www.pewtrusts.org/en/projects/financial-security-and-mobility
http://www.pewtrusts.org/en/about/news-room/press-releases/2008/05/29/new-study-on-economic-opportunity-finds-that-americans-experience-upward-economic-mobility-but-for-many-the-magnitude-of-their-movement-is-minimal, consulted November 29, 2014.

Bonilla-Silva, Eduardo, "The Invisible Weight of Whiteness: The Racial Grammar of Everyday Life in Contemporary America," *Ethnic and Racial Studies*, 2012, 35:2, 173-194

Daehl, Joshua, "Police Killings Call for New Kind of Prosecutor," *Bloomberg View*, December 4, 2014 http://www.bloombergview.com/articles/2014-12-04/police-killings-call-for-new-kind-of-prosecutor

Dee, Thomas S., "The Race Connection: Are Teachers More Effective with Students Who Share Their Ethnicity?" *Education Next*, Spring 2004 / vol. 4, no. 2, http://educationnext.org/the-race-connection/

Fields, Carlos, " Award-Winning Community Policing Strategies, 1999-2006, A Report for the International Association of Chiefs of Police," Community Policing Committee, *U.S. Department of Justice*, COPS (Community Oriented Policing Services), http://ric-zai-inc.com/Publications/cops-w0451-pub.pdf

Fredrickson, Darin D. and Raymond P. Siljander *Racial Profiling*, Springfield, IL: Charles C. Thomas, 2002, NCJRS Library Abstracts, http://www.ncjrs.gov/App/publications/abstract.aspx?ID=195100

Gordon, Lewis R., "The Problem with Affirmative Action," Op-Ed, *TruthOut*, August 2011, http://www.s4.brown.edu/us2010/News/inthenews.PDFs/Jul_Aug.2011/us2010news.2011.08.15.truthout.pdf

Harris, Leonard, "'Believe It or Not' or the Ku Klux Klan and American Philosophy Exposed," *Proceedings and Addresses of the American Philosophical Association*, vol. 68, no. 5 (May 1995): pp. 133-137

Haslanger, Sally, "Social Meaning and Philosophic Method," *Proceedings and Addresses of the American Philosophical Association*, vol. 88, November 2014, pp. 16-30

Lever, Annabelle, "Why Racial Profiling Is Hard To Justify: A Response To Risse and Zeckhauser," *Philosophy and Public Affairs* 33(1) (2005): pp. 94–110

Lowrey, Annie, "Big Study Links Good Teachers to Lasting Gain." *New York Times*. January 6, 2012. http://www.nytimes.com/2012/01/06/education/big-study-links-good-teachers-to-lasting-gain.html?pagewanted=all. For the study itself, see Raj Chetty, John N. Friedman, and Jonah E. Rockoff, "The Long-Term Impacts of Teachers: Teacher Value-Added and Student Outcomes in Adulthood," Columbia University and NBER.http://obs.rc.fas.harvard.edu/chetty/value_added.html, (both consulted on November 29, 2014

Malcolm X Grassroots Movement, "Operation Ghetto Storm: 2012 Annual Report on the Extrajudicial Killing of 313 Black People," http://mxgm.org/operation-ghetto-storm-2012-annual-report-on-the-extrajudicial-killing-of-313-black-people/, May 2013

McIntosh, Peggy "White Privilege: Unpacking the Invisible Backpack," 1989. http://www.deanza.edu/faculty/lewisjulie/White%20Priviledge%20Unpacking%20the%20Invisible%20Knapsack.pdf

Mills, Charles W., "Rawls on Race/Race in Rawls," *Southern Journal of Philosophy* vol. XLVII (2009): pp. 160-185

Osborne, Jason W., "Testing Stereotype Threat: Does Anxiety Explain Race and Sex Differences in Achievement?" *Contemporary Educational Psychology*, vol. 26, no. 3 (July 2001): pp. 291–310

Outlaw, Lucius, "Africana Philosophy," in *The Stanford Encyclopedia of Philosophy*, October, 2010, http://plato.stanford.edu/entries/africana/

Peralta, Eyder and Krishnadev Calamur, "Ferguson Documents: How the Grand Jury Reached a Decision," *The Two-Way*, NPR.ORG, November 25, 2014, http://www.npr.org/blogs/thetwo-way/2014/11/25/366507379/ferguson-docs-how-the-grand-jury-reached-a-decision

Phelps, Elizabeth A., "Race, Behavior, and the Brain: The Role of Neuroimaging in Understanding Complex Social Behaviors," *Political Psychology*, vol. 24, no. 4, Special Issue: *Neuroscientific Contributions to Political Psychology* (December 2003): pp. 747-758

Reaves, Brian A. "Census of State and Local Law Enforcement Agencies," Bureau of Justice Statistics, U.S. Department of Justice, http://bjs.ojp.usdoj.gov/content/pub/pdf/csllea08.pdf

Shelby, Tommie "Justice, Deviance, and the Dark Ghetto," *Philosophy & Public Affairs*, vol. 35, no. 2 (Spring 2007): pp. 126–160

United Nations Committee Against Torture (CAT), http://www.ohchr.org/EN/HRBodies/CAT/Pages/CATIndex.aspx

United Nations, "Universal Declaration of Human Rights" http://www.un.org/en/documents/udhr/index.shtml#ap

Zack, Naomi, "Philosophical Theories of Justice, Inequality, and Racial Inequality," *Graduate Faculty Philosophy Journal*, Special Issue on Race in the History of Philosophy, New School University (2014): pp. 353-368

_____, "Racial Inequality and a Theory of Applicative Justice," *Philosophy and the Black Experience, The American Philosophical Association Newsletter*, vol. 13, no. 1 (Fall 2013): pp. 6-11

NEWS

News articles were referred to from the following sources, February 2012 to December 2014:

BREITBART.com, http://www.breitbart.com
CBS News/AP, http://www.cbsnews.com/news/
CNN, http://www.cnn.com
The Examiner, www.sfexaminer.com
International Business Times,. http://www.ibtimes.com
The Guardian, http://www.theguardian.com
Huffington Post, http://www.huffingtonpost.com
New York Daily News.Com, http://www.nydailynews.com
NPR.ORG, http://www.npr.org
NYTimes, http://www.nytimes.com
Rolling Out, http://rollingout.com
USA Today, http://www.usatoday.com
Wall Street Journal, http://www.wsj.com
World News Group, www.worldmag.com

OTHER SOURCES

Blackpast.Org. "The Black Laws of Oregon, 1844-1857," http://www.blackpast.org/perspectives/black-laws-oregon-1844-1857
Legal Information Institute, Cornell University, http://www.law.cornell.edu/
"List of Police Television Drama," *Wikipedia*, http://en.wikipedia.org/wiki/List_of_police_television_dramas
Oregon, State and County Quickfacts, U.S. Census, http://quickfacts.census.gov/qfd/states/41000.html
Prison Policy.org, http://www.prisonpolicy.org/global/
Stinson, Philip M., (Criminological Studies), http://works.bepress.com/philip_stinson/
Tamir Rice's Autopsy report, Coyahoga County Medical Examiner's Office, Case Number IN2014-01991 http://media.newsnet5.com/uploads/Tamir-Rice-Autopsy-Report-121214.pdf
U.S. Census, Vintage 2008 data http://www.census.gov/popest/data/historical/2000s/vintage_2008/
U.S. Government, *Our Documents*, http://www.ourdocuments.gov/doc.php?flash=true&doc=97

INDEX

ABOUT THE AUTHOR

Naomi Zack received her PhD in philosophy from Columbia University and is professor of philosophy at the University of Oregon. Her latest book is *The Ethics and Mores of Race: Equality after the History of Philosophy* (2011, 2015). Zack's recent books are *Ethics for Disaster* (2009, 2010), *Inclusive Feminism: A Third Wave Theory of Women's Commonality* (2005) and *The Handy Answer Philosophy Book* (2010). Zack's earlier books include: *Race and Mixed Race* (1993); *Bachelors of Science* (1996); *Philosophy of Science and Race* (2002), and the short textbook, *Thinking About Race* (2nd edition, 2006). Zack's book in progress is *The Theory of Applicative Justice: A Pragmatic Approach to Correcting Injustice.* Zack also organizes the project on home and homelessness for the University of Oregon Philosophy Department, including the multimedia website: http://homelessness.philosophy. uoregon.edu/.